THE RIGHT WAY

A guide for parents and teachers to encourage visual learners

by

ELAINE L. LOWENBERG

M.A., D.Litt et Phil.

and

ELSIE M. LUCAS

D.O.T.(Pret), D.S.E.(Unisa), B.A.(Natal)

GECKO BOOKS

First published in 1996 by T E L Publishers
This edition published in 1999
by Gecko Books, 21 Hereward Road, Umbilo, Durban 4001, South Africa

© Elaine Lowenberg and Elsie Lucas

ISBN 1 875011 26 9

Cover design: Hazell Munro
Typesetting by Alpha Typesetters cc, New Germany, KwaZulu-Natal
Printed and bound by Kohler Carton & Print, Pinetown

THE RIGHT WAY

A guide for parents and teachers
to encourage visual learners

DEDICATION

This book is dedicated to our colleague and close friend, Clarice Tucker, who was well known to many in South Africa for her untiring effort in providing opportunities and facilities for left handers. Clarice was the one person who made frequent contact urging us to complete the book but regrettably, her enthusiastic request for the first autographed copy was not to be, as she passed away before this could be achieved.

Foreword

MANY years ago, before any thoughts of right hemisphere dominance had crossed my mind, or had been mentioned in research, I was acutely aware of the differing cognitive styles amongst pupils. When school principals and inspectors rate teachers, a major factor to take into account has always been their competency to cope with a wide spectrum of abilities, personalities and learning styles amongst the thirty or more pupils in a class. Our weakest teachers tend to regard a class as a homogenous whole.

The authors have pioneered research in a longitudinal study of hemisphere dominance for over two decades in South Africa, involving hundreds of pupils, with as much emphasis on the practical application of dealing with a situation as on identification. This is of inestimable value to parents and teachers. The purpose of this book, therefore, is to sensitise all concerned to the educational needs of the pupils described.

Experience at many levels in the education system, from teachers to administrators, convinces me that where indicated, once the relevant materials and strategies are used in the classroom between Grade One and Grade Seven, such pupils will be applying visual learning techniques for themselves by the time they reach high school and many of their problems will be resolved. I therefore urge Grade One to Grade Three teachers in particular and teachers in Senior Primary phase in general, to read and discuss the content of this book, which gives a user friendly step by step guide on how to ensure that our visual learner does not become a problem pupil due to years of frustration and under-achievement. The liberal use of illustrations are particularly helpful for visual thinkers.

Not only is the six to twelve year age group the optimum time to resolve problems, but, teachers in the primary schools are particularly well equipped to deal with the situation, because as class teachers they are working with the pupil for most of the day, which offers a great deal more flexibility and input across all of the curriculum. High school teachers are also urged to familiarise themselves with the strategies used, as sadly, all too frequently, the comment on school reports, "must work harder", is regarded as the sole panacea for resolving genuine learning problems of all types.

It is also important that parents familiarise themselves with the problems faced by visual learners in the learning situation. The parents are then able to empathise with the child and co-operate constructively with the school, especially in the development of good behaviour and work habits. The teacher is often the mother figure in the classroom, especially with young pupils.

The Right Way is the product of considerable research and experience in a South African setting, which has brought us up to date with research elsewhere in the Western world. In this regard we owe a great deal of gratitude to the authors.

Joe Siney
Director Educent Remedial Clinic

Contents

Acknowledgements

THE material in this book is based on the work done by the authors over the past twenty years in the KwaZulu-Natal area. It has become a reality because of the help and co-operation of a large number of children, parents and families too numerous to mention here by name. Our sincere thanks and appreciation to the many classroom teachers and school principals who have supported us over the years. We are indebted to friends and colleagues, in particular Joe Siney, whose experience we appreciate, as well as his willing response when he was approached to write our foreword. To Hazell Munro, who is herself a visual learner, whose talents in art were not recognised in school but speak volumes within these covers, where each of her drawings convey a message far stronger than many pages of text. To Lorraine Williams for her contribution at such very short notice and at a difficult time in her busy life. For their encouragement and patience we thank our families, Josh Goldberg for his understanding, advice and plain common sense. To Terry Tuck for many hours spent on the original draft, without him this work would not have been completed. Finally, to Dr Rose Morris, whose contribution resulted in several positive changes and finalisation of the manuscript.We also acknowledge with gratitude the contributions from the following: Drs L I Robertson and Bhagwan, Professors Betty Edwards, A Lasich, D K Turnbull and Messrs Tony Enslin, Paulette du Bayle-Barker, Shirley Bell, Patricia Rudden, Carol Herbert, Hazel Imber, Mary Hudson, Jayishree Singh, Rita Edwards and Sheila Tuck.

Elaine Lowenberg and Elsie Lucas

Introduction

YOUNG children, especially pre-schoolers, are the world's best scholars. Motivated, active, keen and enthusiastic are apt descriptions for these little people. Unfortunately, these qualities are short-lived for some, the right-brain visual learners, who, when they leave the comfortable creative environment of the pre-primary school, soon discover that

"WHEN EDUCATION STARTS, LEARNING STOPS"

There are very few educators who feel confident enough to say

"If the child is not learning from the way I teach, then I should try to teach in the way the child learns."

In this guide, the authors have endeavoured to present suggestions that should make it easier for parents and teachers to create learning opportunities that will lead to right-brain visual learners realising their potential.

When the authors made their decision to share their experiences of the past twenty years with visual learners and their families, they opted for a guide with a practical content, in order to reach as many parents, teachers and colleagues as possible.

As there are many more boys than girls who are visual learners, the term "he" has been used in general, although the examples given apply equally to boys and girls.

In this guide, Part 1 outlines the development of the brain as it relates to learning, describes the characteristics of the visual learner and provides insight into the expected behaviour and levels of performance at differing age levels. Reading Part 1 will make it easier to apply the practical information provided in Part 2 appropriately.

In Part 2, behavioural management and basic principles of teaching are discussed, together with special techniques to promote the development of basic skills for learning, as well as to teach strategies to improve performance in reading, writing, phonics, spelling and written language, and maths. Some suggestions are included for teachers to help the visual learner in the classroom. There is also a chapter focusing on creative study methods which can be used effectively with senior primary and high school children.

Finally, there are a large number of left-handers in the population of visual learners and because many visual learners have an Attention Deficit Disorder (ADD), the last two chapters provide information relating to these two topics.

To the parent

We are aware that parents are blamed but not trained. Because it is assumed that child rearing is a natural phenomenon, and every mother has her own built-in knowledge of the child's capabilities and levels of development, we end up with anxious parents and children who cannot cope at school. Then we have the audacity to say that the child has a learning disability, his parents don't know how to handle him, he is so spoiled. The reality is that parents try their best and through lack of knowledge, guidelines and a lack of help, often find that their good intentions do not translate into positive changes in their child's behaviour or learning. It is our hope that when parents have read this book, the above situation could be reversed by

HELPING THEM TO HAVE MORE CONFIDENCE IN THEMSELVES AND THEIR CHILDREN

To the teacher

If you are a self-motivated, dedicated teacher, maybe a visual learner yourself, consider the following challenge:

If you have any children in your class whom the school system regards as hopeless and unteachable, maybe you can see them as youngsters with potential and dreams. When others have given up on them, maybe you can fight for their right to give them the two best things a teacher can bestow on any of her pupils,

HOPE AND BELIEF IN THEMSELVES

PART 1

WHO IS THIS CHILD?

CHAPTER 1

The Brain and Learning

IN the last few years there has been a marked increase in the amount of research relating to specialised functions of the two hemispheres of the brain. Some of these findings are having an observable impact on education.

There are specific and positive implications for visual learners, a good example being the new approach to learning mathematics, which has been introduced into South African schools. As the new maths is a system which provides ample opportunities for visual learners to experience success when doing mathematical calculations, a brief description of this exciting development in education is included in Chapter 6.

There is now more awareness of the need to encourage whole brain learning, where previously Western cultures concentrated mainly on developing the left hemisphere, whilst the East seemed to be providing more opportunities for right brain learners.

An infant is born with a full complement of brain cells, as yet undeveloped, with rapid growth taking place from the fourth to fourteenth week of pregnancy. In the event of brain injury in a young child, the intact hemisphere can take over the functions of the defective side, before the cells have become committed.

Initially a baby learns from what he sees and later attaches language labels. As visual learning precedes language learning it is, at least in the early stages of the learning process, the more efficient system for immediate learning to take place. The visual stimulus remains intact, whilst the auditory stimulus is often, due to attention wandering, lost, allowing no time to re-focus before it disappears.

According to Professor M D N Murphy, in his book "The Greatest Adventure", neurologists, neurosurgeons and psychologists were surprised to discover that the brain had two distinct hemispheres, the left side controlling thinking processes and the right side controlling intuition.

The human brain consists of two halves, similar in appearance and convoluted to contain billions of nerve cells. They are called the left and right hemispheres and are connected to the nervous system in a cross-over fashion, with the left hemisphere controlling the right side of the body and the right hemisphere controlling the left side. As a consequence, a stroke in the left side of the brain results in the right side of the body being affected and vice-versa.

As the right hand is controlled by the left hemisphere and the left hand by the right hemisphere, the majority of left handers are right brain dominant.

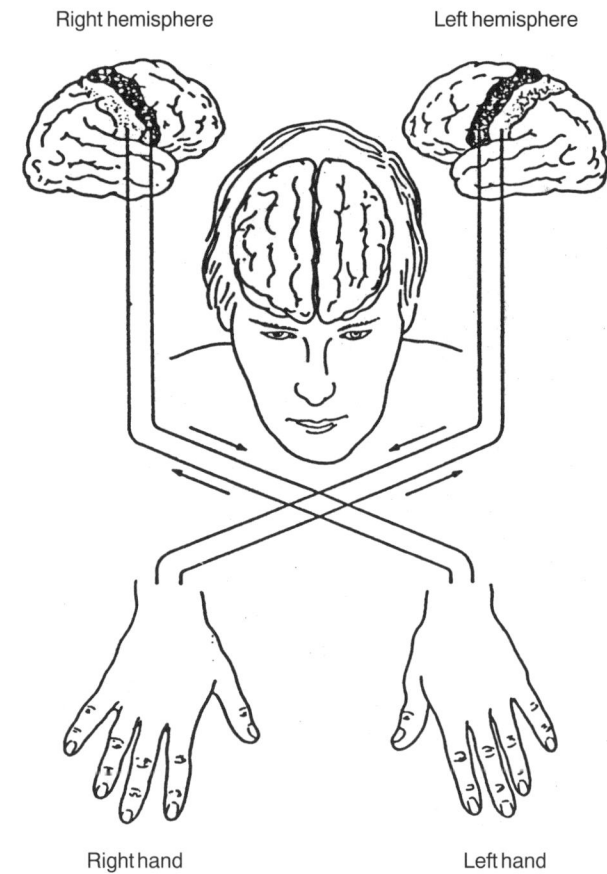

Right hemisphere   Left hemisphere

Right hand   Left hand

Figure 1: *Each hand is served by the cerebral hemisphere on the opposite side.*

Although the two hemispheres are similar in appearance, they are not symmetrical in function. The main language centre is usually situated in the left hemisphere, irrespective of right or left brain dominance, which is the reason why mankind is thought to be left brain dominant. The two hemispheres are connected by a band of nerve fibres called the corpus callosum, which provides communication between the two hemispheres and transmits memory and learning. It allows for specialisation in the two halves of the brain, which are able to complement each other in their complex and different ways of processing information. If the corpus callosum is severed, the two halves of the brain continue to function independently.

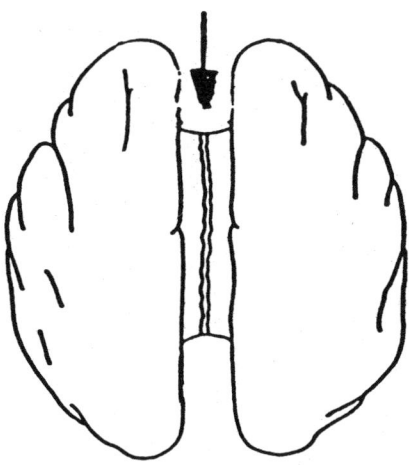

Figure 2: *The corpus callosum connects the two hemispheres of the brain.*

Sperry said, "There appear to be two modes of thinking, verbal and non-verbal, represented rather separately in the right and left hemispheres respectively. Our educational system, as well as science in general, tends to neglect the non-verbal form of intellect. What it comes down to is that modern society discriminates against the right hemisphere".

However, the second world war gave neuro-surgeons the opportunity to learn more about the brain, through the surgical treatment of head injuries. Before this, little attention had been given to visual learning.

Sperry, who won the Nobel Prize for his work in split-brain surgery, found that intractable epilepsy, resulting from serious head injury which did not respond to medication, could be controlled by severing the corpus callosum. From his work, Sperry established that the same information is received by both sides of the brain but is processed differently, namely, in language on the left side and visually on the right, thus:

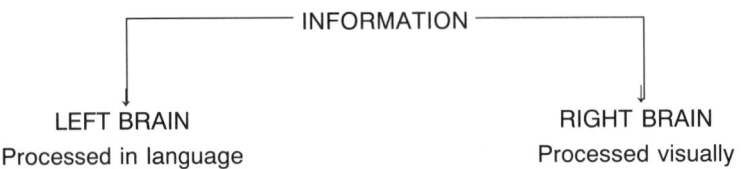

| LEFT BRAIN | RIGHT BRAIN |
| Processed in language | Processed visually |

Example: Both sides of the brain involve thinking, reasoning and complex mental functioning in their own way. In a specially designed test which demonstrates this, two pictures were flashed on a screen, at which a split-brain patient fixed his eyes at the mid-point, to prevent scanning the images. A picture of a spoon on the left side of the screen went to the right side of the brain, and a knife, on the right side of the screen, to the verbal, left side of the brain.

When asked to name what he had seen, he said "a knife", but when asked to pick out the object from a group of objects with his left hand (right brain) from behind a screen, he picked out the spoon.

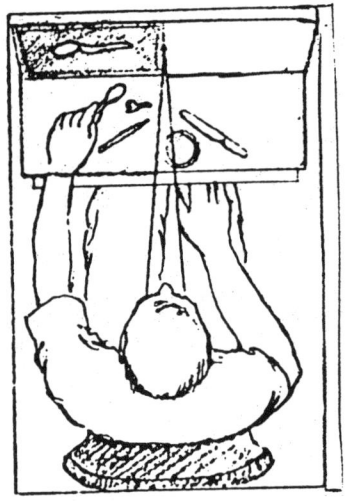

Figure 3: *The effect of split-brain surgery*

The right brain visual learners do not have well developed verbal expressive ability. They have poorly developed concepts of time and they also experience difficulty in sequencing, categorising and labelling, all of which are left-brain skills needed to cope in our left brain orientated school system. Betty Edwards, in her book, "Drawing on the Right Side of the Brain", said, "The right brain is largely untaught". There is glaring evidence in our schools to support her view, as there are few music classes and limited opportunities for children to use imagery, visualisation, spatial skills, or creative talents in the classroom.

6

Many visual learners are spatially competent, with their well developed spatial ability, described by Dr I Macfarlane Smith, as "the psychological opposite of verbal ability, a pervasive trait similar in importance to such traits as verbal or social intelligence. People with this ability are competent in non-verbal directions, namely the technical and mechanical skills required for industrial occupations, but deficiencies in the verbal area handicap their educational and vocational advancement".

This is exemplified by Tom, now aged 53, who has superior intelligence and was admitted to a special class and then to trade school. Mike, aged 25, with above average intelligence, was constantly punished for being 'lazy'. He attended an Afrikaans Medium School as this was the only place to accommodate him, despite his mother tongue being English. Both these men left school at the Grade IX level and became artisans, even although both of them had the potential for tertiary education.

It is now known that a substantial number of right handers are also right brain dominant and research has shown that the areas that control language and related skills are, in some individuals, more evenly distributed between the left and right hemispheres.

After dominance becomes established one has a dominant hand, foot and eye, not necessarily on the same side. For example, one can be left footed and right handed. There is also a dominant, or more efficient way to learn, namely, visually, by means of pictures, shapes and figures, or auditorally, through language.

Since visual perception and visual memory are located in the right cerebral hemisphere, we describe visual learners as right brain dominant, or more correctly, predominant. They appear to see things as a whole, whereas the left-brain dominant people think logically, in a more linear fashion.

LEFT BRAIN-LANGUAGE	RIGHT BRAIN-VISUAL
Linear thinking	Sees the whole
Analytical thinking	Awareness of touch
Hand writing	Spatial relationships
Language	Shapes and patterns
Reading	Colour awareness
Phonics	Music and singing
Locating facts	Creativity
Talking and reciting	Maths computations
Following directions	Visualisation
Listening	Feelings and emotions

Some careers followed are:

LEFT BRAIN
lawyers, accountants
teachers, academics

RIGHT BRAIN
artisans, musicians
engineers, artists

Both sides of the brain work together but one side is predominant, in that it functions more efficiently and more quickly. The dominant side may interfere with non-dominant processing, creating difficulties in both social adjustment and learning.

The neurological components and language processing that take place in the brain are extremely complex. The authors feel that, for this guide, the following simplified description should suffice:-

The majority of people have two language centres, situated in the temporal lobe of the left hemisphere. The first, Broca's Area, controls articulation and mechanical speech, whilst the other, Wernicke's Area, is responsible for language processing and comprehension.

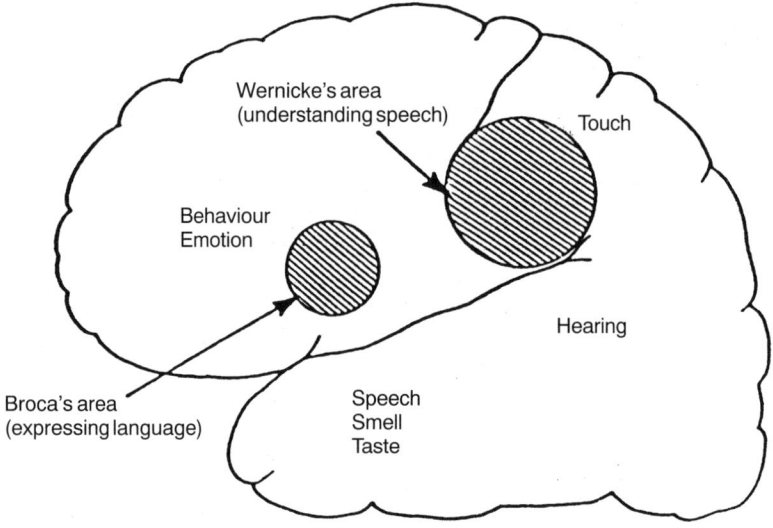

Figure 4: *Side view of the language areas in the left hemisphere of the brain.*

It is the inefficient functioning of Wernicke's Area in some visual learners which accounts for parents being surprised to hear that their child, "who speaks so well", has a weak vocabulary and is slow to understand the spoken word. Some of these children also experience difficulty with written expression and are sometimes labelled "learning disabled".

The left brain has always been accepted as the dominant hemisphere because it contains the major speech areas, but the right brain is in no way inferior and is able to take over left brain functions in the early years of development. This has been shown by brain surgery performed by paediatric neurologists in the U.S.A. on children with a rare condition called Rasmussens Encephalitis. An example is that of a four year old boy whose complete left hemisphere was removed and yet, with therapy, he now speaks normally, copes at school, is doing particularly well in maths and enjoys playing the piano.

Ideally, an integrated whole brain approach to learning is advocated. However, our educational system makes use of teaching techniques which are language loaded, and which favour the child who has better left brain skills, namely, the auditory learner.

Research findings do not always benefit children because they often lack practical implications. Some valuable work has been done by Sandra F Witelson at the Ontario University on left-right processes. She reported that; "Dyslexia may be associated with representation of spatial data (including alphabet letters) in both hemispheres, instead of primarily in the right as is the usual case".

Her studies showed that spatial functions in dyslexic children and some visual learners with reading difficulties are represented bi-laterally. She says that spatial perception could "affect cognition by overloading one hemisphere (the left in this case) and interfering with those functions 'native' to it".

Left hemisphere functions include sequential and linguistic processing and interfering with such processes could negatively influence the performance of linguistic tasks, including reading.

Because spatial processing appears to be represented bi-laterally, Witelson says "that it may be possible to design an appropriate approach to reading that elicits an optimum balance between linguistic processing (the phonetic approach, or, the spatial processing "look-say" method) which may allow dyslexics to progress in reading".

The most efficient practioners are those who not only have a sound theoretical base from which to work but are able to apply the theoretical knowledge appropriately. We have seen instances where valuable time and energy have been lost through inappropriate intervention programmes. The following example is given with the permission of the therapist involved, who expressed the hope that others would benefit from the mistakes that she had made.

She tested a young boy on a memory test of the type where letters written on a card are exposed for a limited time, after which he must make an appropriate response, recalling and naming the letters. He made errors and was assumed to have a poor visual memory which she said accounted for his inability to copy correctly from the blackboard in the class-room.

He commenced training, having extended practice sessions with recalling pictures in their correct sequence. She was surprised how well he responded, but nonetheless continued until he was able to recall up to six pictures in sequence correctly. She then approached his class teacher and was disappointed to hear that his school work had shown no improvement. What had happened was, that when she assessed him, she had not taken into account that letters are not clear visual symbols, but also have sounds. The processing relating to letters is a function of the left hemisphere, whilst pictures are processed on the right. Consequently, training, using letters rather than pictures, would have been more appropriate.

The example below illustrates how a young child processes information;

If a card with p m k t written on it is exposed visually for a limited time, and he is asked to recall it and say what he has seen, he may respond with p m c t. The symbols are recognised visually (right brain processing) and immediately converted to sound (left brain processing). Auditory-visual integration takes place, involving both hemispheres and the 'c' is substituted for 'k' because it appears more frequently in English.

The example shows the complexity of brain processing and emphasises the folly in trying to isolate functions into being confined to a right or left brain process. The ability to learn is dependent on effective integration, association, and whole brain processing, in which both hemispheres are actively involved.

Therapists need to be on the lookout for research studies to ensure that they are providing appropriate and effective intervention for their children. For example, there are many research studies to show that children are sometimes tested on a test such as the "Beery Test of Visual Motor Integration" or the "Frostig Developmental Test of Visual Perception" and having scored poorly, are given appropriate training to improve the skills that are lacking. When they are re-tested they show good gains in test scores, only for the therapist to find that there has been no improvement in their school work.

The implication is that the children have been taught splinter skills, which are often not the same skills needed in the performance of classroom tasks. They have actually only been taught to perform better on the tests.

The ideal solution would be for research and field workers to combine their efforts and continue to work together until their findings have been tested to the point where there is positive feed-back from the children and their teachers.

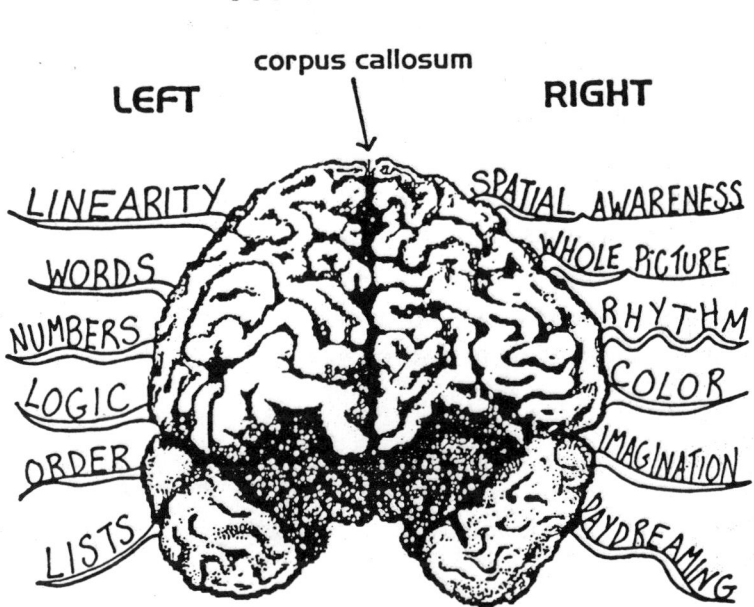

Figure 5: *Visual illustration of hemispheric specialisation.*

CHAPTER 2

Developmental Stages

THE areas of development selected as relevant for this guide are in three categories;

Motor and language levels

Developmental stages of play

Development of academic learning; reading, writing, maths.

WHY ARE NORMS IMPORTANT?

A knowledge of developmental sequences can be helpful to provide information regarding how much of a challenge a child needs, and can also ensure that expectations are not unrealistic.

Here are two examples. Whilst a temper tantrum should never be condoned, it is none-the-less age appropriate behaviour for a three year old but is totally unacceptable in a seven year old.

Figure 1: *"You are 7 years old and capable of finding your own shoes".*

A four year old can copy a square but not a diamond, because the mastery of diagonal line drawing develops much later. On the other hand, if an eight year old has difficulty copying the diamond, he could be regarded as immature in his ability to cope with that particular task (diamond copying), since the majority of eight year olds can copy a diamond correctly.

Awareness of norms, particularly relating to behaviour, can reduce parental anxiety as there will be a realisation that certain negative behaviours are "a passing phase".

It is essential that parents, teachers, therapists and others are cautioned against the temptation to use the norms presented here as a rigid standard of expectancy.

Example: A parent should never say, "My child ought to be at this level because he is old enough".

These norms should not be used to rate children but should rather be seen as useful tools to be used by parents and teachers to guide the child and help him realise his full potential.

In order to protect these norms from arbitrary application, and, at the risk of sounding repetitive, it is again reiterated that there is a need for parents and teachers to constantly remind themselves that individual differences exist in children's development at all levels.

MOTOR DEVELOPMENT

Arnold Gesell, in his book "The Child from Five to Ten" said, "The motor characteristics of every child are worthy of observation because they are indicators of individuality and maturity status".

Posture is regarded as a key concept for interpreting a child's development but should be taken further to include muscle tone and development of fine motor control, eye-hand co-ordination and eye movements.

Opportunities to move and explore are essential for every child to grow and learn. Whilst physical activity is more pronounced in a young child at the pre-primary level, many older children already at school are constantly on the move, this being particularly so if they are right brain, visual learners.

The tragedy is that opportunities to move in our educational system are usually restricted to physical education lessons. Few teachers are assertive, creative or innovative enough to introduce movement in academic learning, for example, using jump sheets for teaching spelling, (Appendix, page 148).

At five a child's typical motor behaviour is to move from one location to another, until he settles in a place where his interest is held.

At six, when in grade one, he is often more restless and moves around the classroom, needing reminders to settle or return to his own desk.

At seven, in grade two, he remains in one place for longer periods and is also learning to finish tasks more easily.

At eight, in grade three, group cohesion starts and there is far less opening and closing of desks, with self regulating behaviour, in terms of taking control of motor movements, having matured substantially.

At nine, motor movements are goal directed and not (as at younger levels) just movement for the sake of movement.

LANGUAGE DEVELOPMENT

This subject is too vast to be thoroughly discussed in this guide, but needs to be mentioned because the importance of developing good language and communication skills cannot be over emphasised, since most children experiencing learning difficulties, and many adults who lack confidence, do not have well developed communication and language skills.

Ideally, visual learners should be recognised in early childhood, to give parents and teachers the chance to deliberately create opportunities to expand vocabulary, develop verbal expression and comprehension, as well as helping them to learn to speak clearly.

When a small child has a lisp, or makes errors in articulation, attention should not be focussed on him. For example, some parents will say, "He sounds so cute when he speaks". If there has been this type of negative reinforcement, it will be more difficult to achieve good results with speech therapy or corrective procedures.

The need to know developmental sequences becomes evident when a parent takes a four year old to a speech therapist because he says 'wabbit' for 'rabbit' or 'free' for 'three', only to be told that this is normal for his age level. This is because 'r' and 'th' are some of the last sounds to be acquired, that is, at the six to seven year level. Because of individual differences there will of course be four to five year olds with well developed language skills who do not make these kinds of errors.

As the visual learner is more prone to language lags, he needs to have stories read to him very regularly and also needs to be encouraged to verbalise, with appropriate praise for verbal responses.

Thinking skills can be developed in many everyday situations in the home, for example, if he says, "Ma, where's my library book?", do not say, "You left it lying on the dining room table", rather say, "Can you think where you may have put it?, I'll help you to find it". Using language and encouraging him to communicate verbally guides him to finding it.

A useful rule of thumb is to answer most questions with another question, then follow through by communicating verbally. Develop language rules for the home or class-room. For example, the words, thing, nice, or get, should be taboo and parents should, by enriching their own vocabulary, provide appropriate alternatives.

In conclusion, it is as well to remember that the young child who has well developed language and verbal comprehension skills is less likely to be educationally at risk.

DEVELOPMENT OF PLAY

Play is a natural enjoyable experience which contributes to the childs growth to maturity. An important realisation for parents and teachers is that he does not play because he is too lazy to work. A child engrossed in play will concentrate with his whole being and derive the emotional satisfaction that he cannot get from other forms of activity.

Arnold Gesell said, "A child's play has a developmental logic which does not necessarily fit into our adult preconception".

Parents should not become concerned about a child's pre-occupation with a single toy or with one kind of play, to the exclusion of others. Such obsessions are common, particularly amongst boys aged five to seven who will play endlessly with toy cars or trains, often to the extent that they are unaware of other happenings in their environment. Many young children are also fascinated by water and will spend an inordinate amount of time playing with hosepipes and the like.

Parents need to make concessions when their child plays. For example, if play is destructive, intervention only becomes necessary when the destructiveness becomes violent, emotionally charged, or out of control, which means that he is not yet ready for that level of play and should be encouraged to play more appropriately.

Parents and teachers should also be cautioned against making incorrect interpretations of play. For example, what looks like unreasonable behaviour, such as a little girl jabbing her doll in the stomach, or tearing out it's eyes, is not necessarily a symbolic act of sadism, it could just be practical experimentation.

Because most games and play activities are colour or visually stimulating, or have a physical component, the visual learner is more attracted to those activities, which do not require the use of a paper and pencil, or long periods of sitting, focussing on the same mundane tasks. For example, one little boy, whilst being tested, said, "Can't I rather play one of your games because I hate to work like this for ever and ever". This was despite frequent changes in activities.

Visual learners need challenges and are easily distracted if not visually stimulated.

DEVELOPMENT OF ACADEMIC LEARNING

Reading

A distinction needs to be made between teaching and creating opportunities to learn. Many parents will say, "I feel so guilty because I didn't teach him to read, but it was because his pre-school teacher said that I musn't". If one is sensitive, the child will determine his own needs and all one has to do is respond to his signals.

For example, he may be looking at pictures and words in a book and suddenly say, "What is this word?". Saying the word for him immediately creates the learning opportunity. If, on the other hand, you say, "Look at it and try to sound it out", you are trying to teach him and this can cause confusion and frustration, despite your good intentions.

Encouraging good reading behaviour is important, as he cannot learn to read in isolation. However, even if good remedial help results in him acquiring the skills, the efforts will bear no fruit if he hates books and reading. Attempts to improve reading ability must go hand in glove with developing a positive attitude towards books and their contents.

At 18 months to two years the reading process starts, when the child begins to look at pictures and starts to turn pages in his books. He should be read to for short periods. Books that have rhymes and pictures of familiar objects are the most popular for this age group, for example, Dr Seuss. Allow him to sit on your lap, as physical contact conveys the message that books and love go together.

At three to four he becomes very busy on the physical level as he goes about exploring the whole world. As a consequence, books are not high on his list of priorities at this stage.

16

At four to five he likes to listen to stories about movement, for example, trains, boats and animals that are active.

At five to six he begins to show a preference for certain stories which he wants to have read to him over and over. He loves those about animals that behave like human beings, for example, Winnie the Pooh. He also likes "funny books", for example, Bangers and Mash, the two mischievious monkey brothers.

At six to seven he starts to recognise words. At this stage he is not quite as selective but tends to become disturbed by unpleasant events in stories. This point should be taken seriously in relation to visual learners, as they are often more sensitive than their counterparts. The child now becomes interested in comics and also enjoys memorising stories.

At seven to eight he may already be a fluent reader and enjoys reading at odd times, for example, whilst playing, or he may bring his book to the dinner table. Do not punish him, rather point out that this behaviour is inappropriate, the house rule being that no books or objects not food related, are allowed at the table. He should at the same time be re-assured that you will read with him after the meal.

This is the time when he may enjoy visits to the library. Alice in Wonderland, Peter Pan and Hobbit are examples of popular books for this age group.

At the eight to nine year level reading is, for some children, particularly the girls, a very important pastime. They now start to show an interest in Bible stories and want to know more about adult books.

At nine most children have acquired all the basic skills needed to read fluently. They start to read mysteries, biographies and include magazines and newspapers in their reading schedule. This is when they will begin to buy, borrow, swop and hoard books.

THE VISUAL LEARNER AND READING

There are unfortunately many visual learners who do not follow the developmental sequences described above in their reading behaviour. They tend to start well and remember their flash cards and sight words, because they have well developed visual skills. However, when phonics are introduced they will regress and may only be back on track by grade three or four, with remedial support sometimes being necessary in the interim to help them keep pace with their peers, as well as to maintain a positive attitude towards reading.

DEVELOPMENT OF WRITING

At three and a half to four an interest in writing starts. At this level the child usually has an immature pencil grip but enjoys scribbling. He can draw a rudimentary circle and can sometimes copy a cross, but does not form any letters.

At four to five a square can be copied. He becomes interested in writing capital letters because they are more visually distinctive. He prefers to write the round letters, for example, the C, O and G, because the drawing of circles has been mastered but diagonals are still difficult to do at this stage.

Letters from his own name are preferred and most of the letters are printed very large and randomly on the page. There is also a tendency to write each letter in three to four separate parts.

At five to six he begins to understand how to draw diagonal lines. Letters which he previously wrote in three to four parts are now written in two parts. He attempts to print his own name but the letters are large and irregularly spaced. It is now common for him to start writing small, with letters rapidly increasing in size towards the end of the line.

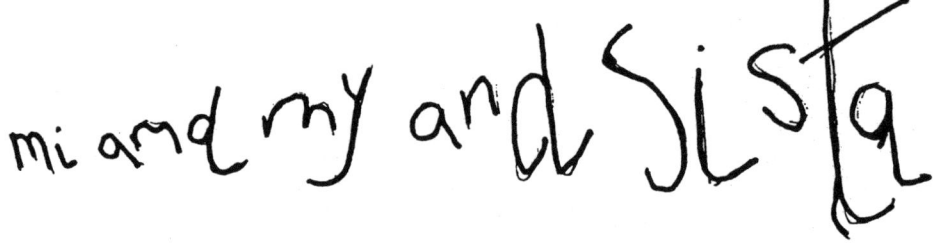

Figure 2: *A sample of writing taken from a seven year old's newsbook.*

The writing of numbers, especially significant ones like his age are now attempted. He starts to copy numbers off the clock or the calendar. Some children will write from right to left but reversals do not occur.

At six to seven he learns to print all the letters and starts to write words. He is now able to make continuous strokes when printing. He starts to experiment with different writing materials and surfaces, for example, he enjoys working on the blackboard.

He uses wax crayons, kokis or pencil crayons interchangeably. His letters are large and uneven, with reversals now occuring, particularly the s, b and d. He enjoys writing numbers but again reversals frequently occur, particularly the 3, 7 and 9.

At seven to eight he has no difficulty printing letters, words and sentences. He starts to distinguish between capital and small letters. He is able to exercise more control over the sizing of his letters.

He prefers using lined paper and starts to use an eraser, as he is becoming conscious of the need to be neat and to avoid errors when writing. Some children, particularly visual learners, prefer to write numbers vertically, rather than horizontally.

At eight to nine he starts to write stories "for fun". Reversals and mirror images are now rare and his spacing between words is regular, with the use of his finger to help him to space no longer being needed.

In the systems where cursive writing is taught, the transition from printing is completed. The children who have learned Nelson (Natalia Script) have now learned to join their letters.

At nine years of age hand writing should have become a useful tool. He is now capable of doing extended periods of writing, with his letters being smaller, neater, evenly spaced and with a slant and individual style now having developed.

As he learns to apply less pressure on his pencil, the speed and volume of his written work increases. The nine year old should have developed to the point where he has acquired all the skills needed to write quickly, spontaneously and neatly.

VISUAL LEARNERS AND WRITING

Because writing is a learned skill, which can only be mastered with constant repetitive practice, the visual learners, who are often physically active and unable to focus their attention for long periods, are not good candidates for learning to write. They are as a consequence often the children who are referred for occupational therapy because their writing is not at the same level as that of their peers.

DEVELOPMENT OF MATHEMATICS

The two major aspects of basic maths concepts are the recognition and manipulation of numbers and secondly the acquisition and application of the language of maths, making it possible to cope with problem solving.

An example of the language of maths includes learning the concepts of more and less. Later, the operations termed addition, subtraction, multiplication and division are learned and even later, the meaning of the words product and the sum of.

At 18 months he can build a tower of four cubes and uses the word **more**.

At two he can distinguish one from many, but cannot count. The idea of **more** is usually conveyed with the words "anuvver one".

At three he can count two objects and although he may be capable of rote counting up to five, he does not understand the one-to-one relationship and is unable to hand over more than two objects on request.

At four he counts by pointing to three objects and rote counting goes to ten, or more.

At five he counts well in ones to thirty and can maintain the one-to-one relationship in his counting to about thirteen. He is able to name certain coins and starts to write numbers. He has no difficulty recognising numbers but does not write them easily yet. It is not unusual to hear a five year old say, "I know it's a seven but I don't know how it looks when I have to write it".

At this stage he enjoys doing basic oral additions but subtraction is virtually impossible.

At six he counts to fifty, or even a hundred but invariably ends on ninety-nine, or the first number that comes to mind. He learns to count in tens and copes with addition and bonds up to ten. Subtraction is more difficult but can be handled up to five.

At seven he counts to one hundred by ones, fives and tens and also to twenty in two's. All coins can be named and numbers can be written from 1 to 20, and higher. He no longer relies on verbal cues to write numbers but mouth movements may be detected as he still counts silently to himself as he writes.

He copes with addition up to twenty and subtraction to ten. He also grasps the meaning of half a unit or a group.

At eight he can count by three's to thirty and by fours to forty. He has mastered most of his bonds and starts with multiplication. He begins to measure distances, showing an interest in peoples weights, as well as the relative values of money. At this stage some children suddenly grasp the concept that multiplication is a series of additions.

At nine he learns about division and has mastered most of the mathematical operations. In addition, most of his multiplication tables have been memorised and can be recalled instantly. He has now acquired the basic skills needed to profit from exposure to mathematical instruction at higher levels.

MATHEMATICS AND THE VISUAL LEARNER

Some visual learners have superior ability to manipulate numbers orally and mentally. School maths requires recorded responses, which are not always up to standard in the visual learner. He may also experience difficulties with the language aspects and may be unable to cope with story sums.

In high school there is a discrepancy in performance between geometry and algebra, in favour of the former, which requires more right brain skills, whilst the latter represents left brain functioning.

IN CONCLUSION

It should be emphasised that maturation cannot be forced. For example, it is unlikely that a mother will take her six month old baby and stand him on his feet in order to teach him to walk, because she is aware that he still has to crawl and stand, before he can walk. By the same token, she should also realise that a four year old cannot be expected to draw a diamond, because he has not yet mastered the drawing of diagonal lines and must first draw squares, and later will learn to draw a diamond.

Sometimes, parents and teachers need guidance from professionals, such as a psychologist, an occupational or speech therapist, who can administer standardised tests to determine whether a child is a visual learner, immature, or has a specific learning disability (see Figures 3 and 4).

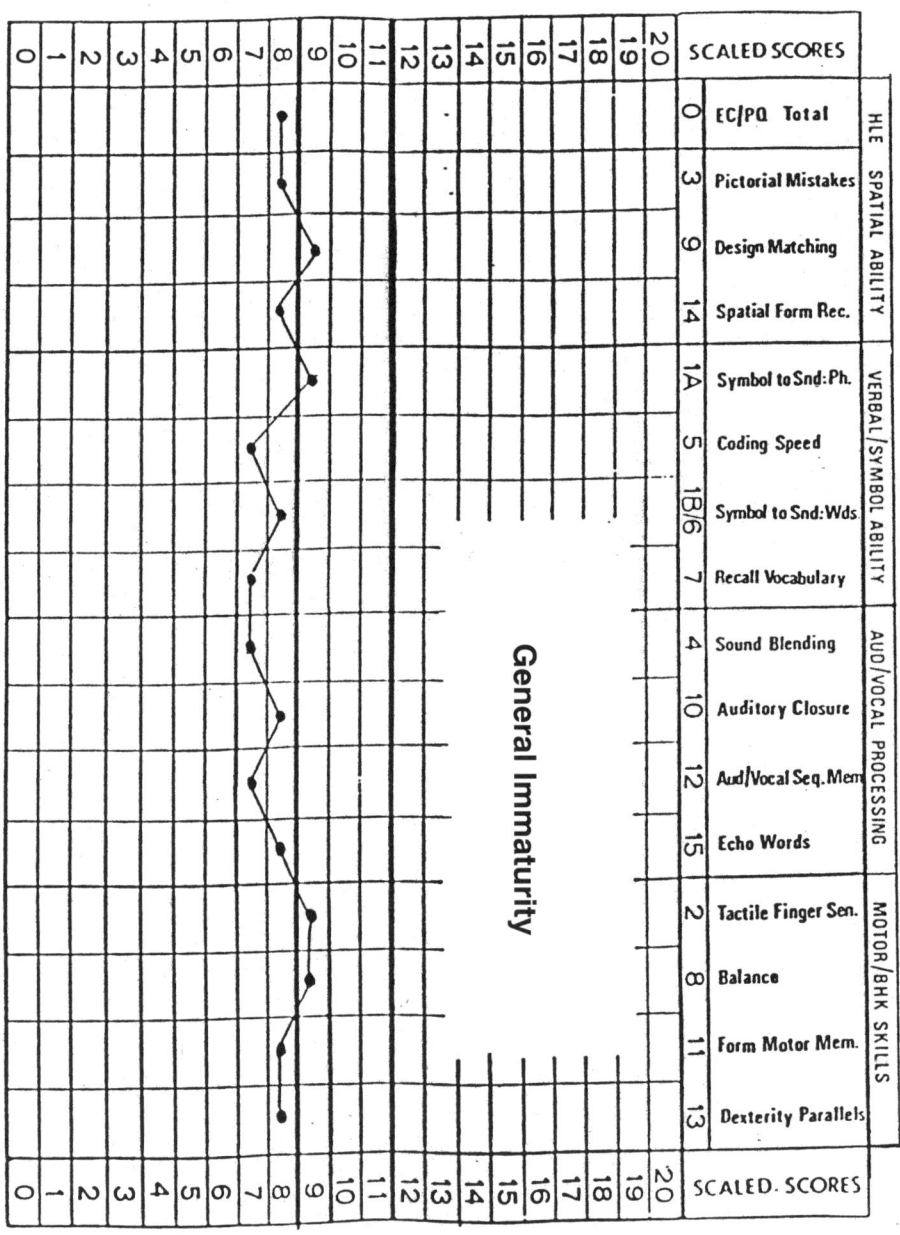

Figure 3: *A graph of a test profile reflecting general immaturity (an even distribution of test scores).*

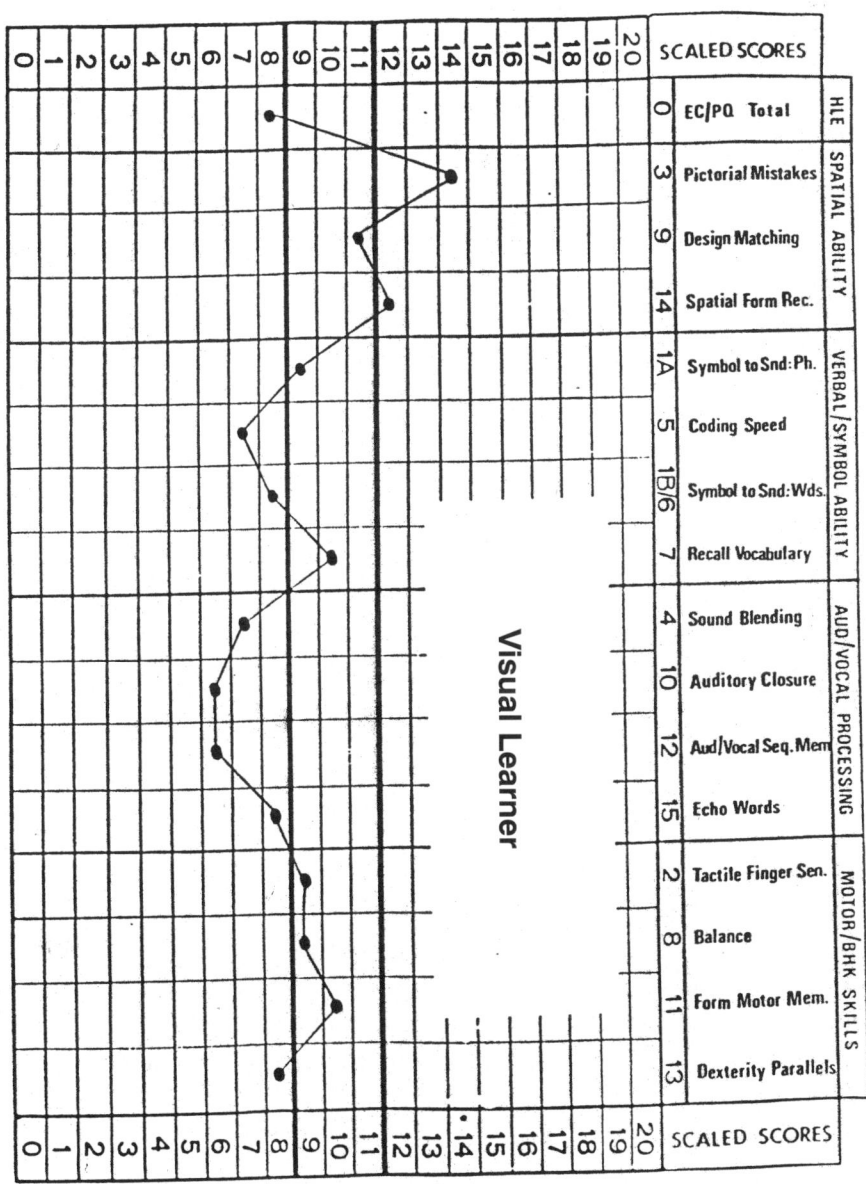

Figure 4: *A graph of a test profile reflecting specific strengths and weaknesses (scatter in test scores).*

CHAPTER 3

Characteristics and Identification of the Visual Learner

CHARACTERISTICS

K NOWING the characteristics of the visual learner makes it possible to accommodate his learning style in an individualised teaching programme. It also ensures that he is taught in a way that he can learn. There is no one specific characteristic or symptom that could be described as sufficient evidence to state that the child is a visual learner.

Figure 1: *Identifying the right brain visual learner.*

However, when several of the following, not necessarily all, classroom, home and behavioural traits are noticed in a particular child, it is time to take a closer look. Before presenting some of the more common traits, we need to emphasize that a teacher should not feel guilty if she does not recognise the visual learner in her classroom, as there is little in the present syllabus to give her guidelines or opportunities to identify these children.

The pre-primary school and the early part of grade one provides a visual learning environment, which is interrupted when the child is faced with a more language orientated learning structure. For example, when phonics are introduced he finds himself unable to make a successful shift to activate left brain functions.

CLASSROOM TRAITS

❑ His performance in phonic based activities is poor.

❑ He experiences difficulty with rote memory, rote counting, saying the alphabet in the correct sequence or memorising multiplication tables.

❑ If verbal instructions are given by the teacher he often resorts to checking what others are doing before commencing his own work.

❑ If the lesson has a high verbal content he is very likely to be the one caught day dreaming.

❑ He resorts to making meaningful substitutions, most noticeable when he reads, for instance, one of our pupils read, "The puppy drinks from his bowl", when the sentence in the book was, "The dog eats from the dish".

❑ Reading may be good but tends to be mechanical, with inaccurate word recognition.

❑ He sometimes guesses, using visual skills by looking at the first letter and shape of the word which results in reading, *carry* for *canary*, *basket* for *biscuit* or *soccer* for *saucer*.

❑ He has difficulty following verbal instructions, particularly when he is required to describe tasks which he usually can perform physically with relative ease.

❑ Concentration varies, with the ability to focus well on tasks which interest him but he is easily distracted when not challenged. This is often related to poor auditory memory, whilst visual memory may be good.

❑ He underachieves in the classroom in language related tasks but copes well with mathematical calculations. His weakness in maths is usually for story sums, where poor reading, listening and an inability to manipulate language concepts are the interfering factors.

❑ He is the child who is restless and disruptive in the classroom because he cannot concentrate and consequently he tends to be frustrated and unmotivated.

❑ "He seems to know just how much he needs to do to keep out of trouble", is the way many teachers and parents describe him.

❑ He has poor concentration at school but not at home, because home based activities are often visual, such as Lego, television, card and video games.

❏ Sequencing is weak. Instead of logical, linear thinking, which is left-brain reasoning, he visualises ideas as a whole. When asked to repeat a story he gives details out of sequence.

❏ If given the digits 1 7 8 6 to repeat, instead of doing so in logical order, he will see them as a whole:

8

1   6

7

and he says, 1 8 7 6.

❏ He is disorganised in the presentation of his work, for example:

The left-brain child, given a sheet of paper on which to draw patterns one at a time, will work from left to right, top to bottom, or in a logical sequence down the page.

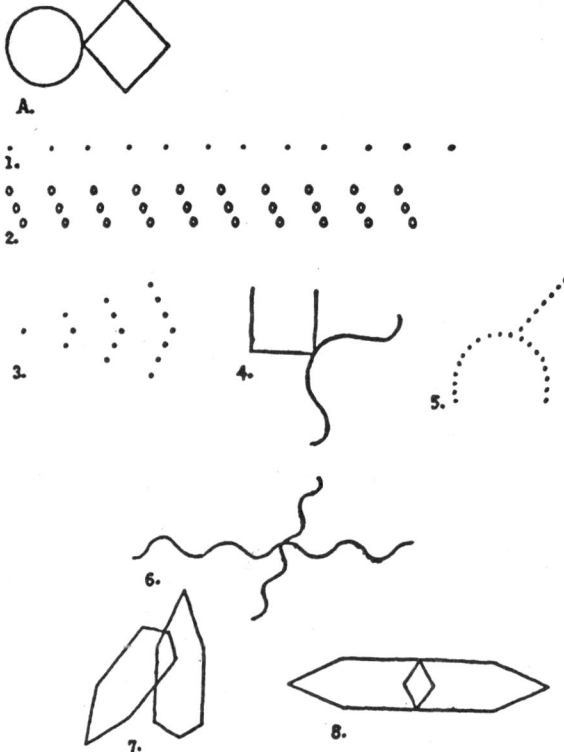

Figure 2: *The left brain child's orderly presentation.*

The visual learner will see the page as a whole and place them in any order.

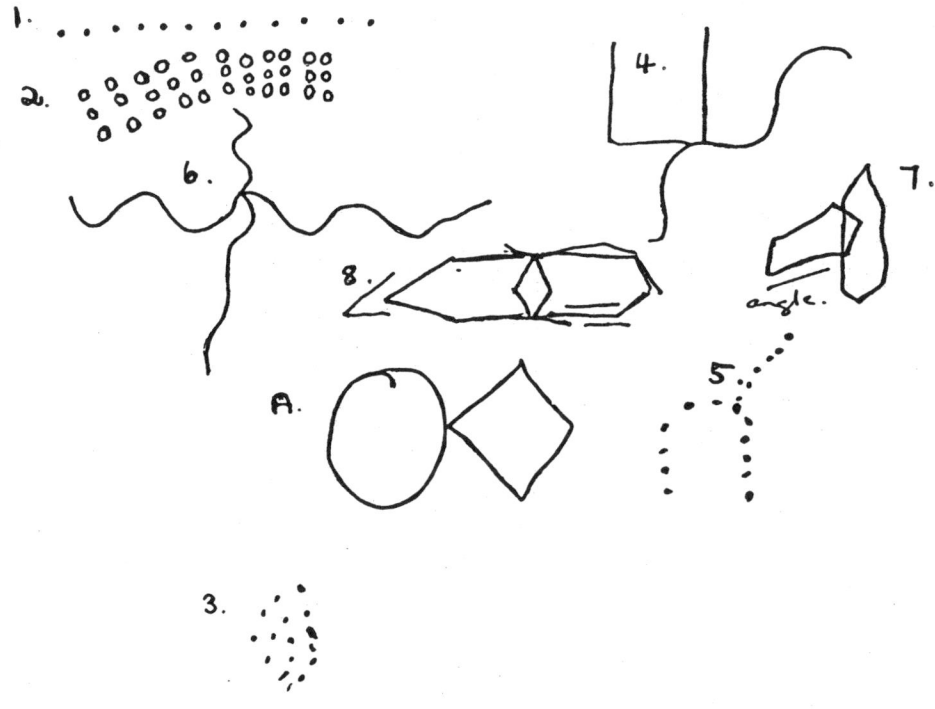

Figure 3: *The right brain child's disorganised presentation.*

☐ An adult visual learner has coined the expression "beaming out" to describe day dreaming. For example, the teacher may use a rabbit to illustrate a point in her story, he "beams out"into his own story about his rabbit and when he "returns", he has missed what the teacher has been saying and gives answers relating to his own rabbit in response to her question.

His performance does not match his potential, that is, he does not seem to be as bright as his test scores indicate on an assessment because he is taught in a language orientated educational system in which he is unable to utilise his non-verbal potential, which is superior to his verbal ability. However, if there is a visual or visual-perceptual disability, there may not be such a significant difference between verbal and non-verbal IQ scores and occupational therapy is required to overcome the problem. Figure 4 reflects the profile of a visual learner where non-verbal IQ score is significantly superior to verbal. Figure 5 also shows the IQ scores of the visual learner but in this case verbal scores are below normal, indicating a specific language disability. Pupils falling into this category are generally transferred to a special class because they are unable to achieve in language skills, such as vocabulary, comprehension and verbal expression, at their age level. Figure 6 shows that the profile does not change in adulthood – once a visual learner, always a visual learner!

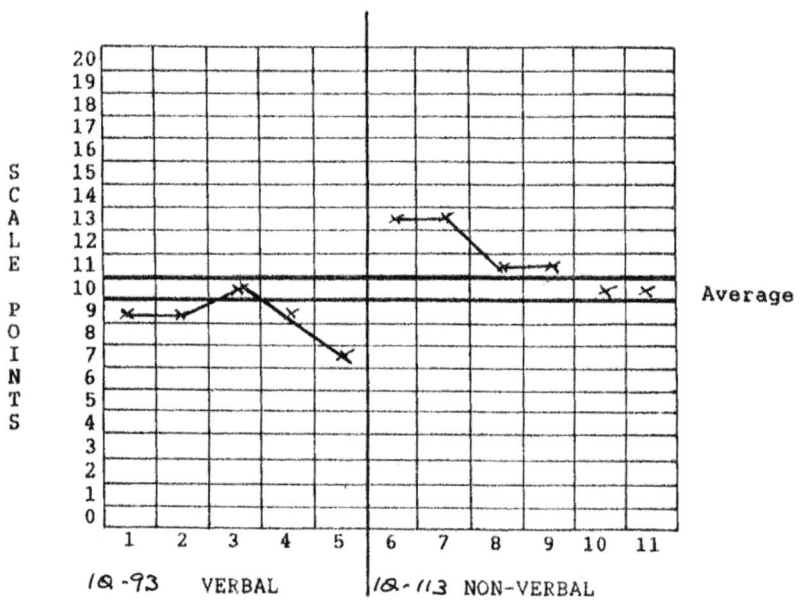

KEY:

1. Vocabulary
2. Comprehension
3. Similarities
4. Number Problems

5. Story Memory
6. Pattern Completion
7. Blocks
8. Missing Parts

9. Form Board
10. Memory for Digits
11. Coding

Figure 4: *A graph of an I.Q. assessment of a visual learner.*

I.Q. TEST
SENIOR SOUTH AFRICAN INDIVIDUAL SCALE – REVISED

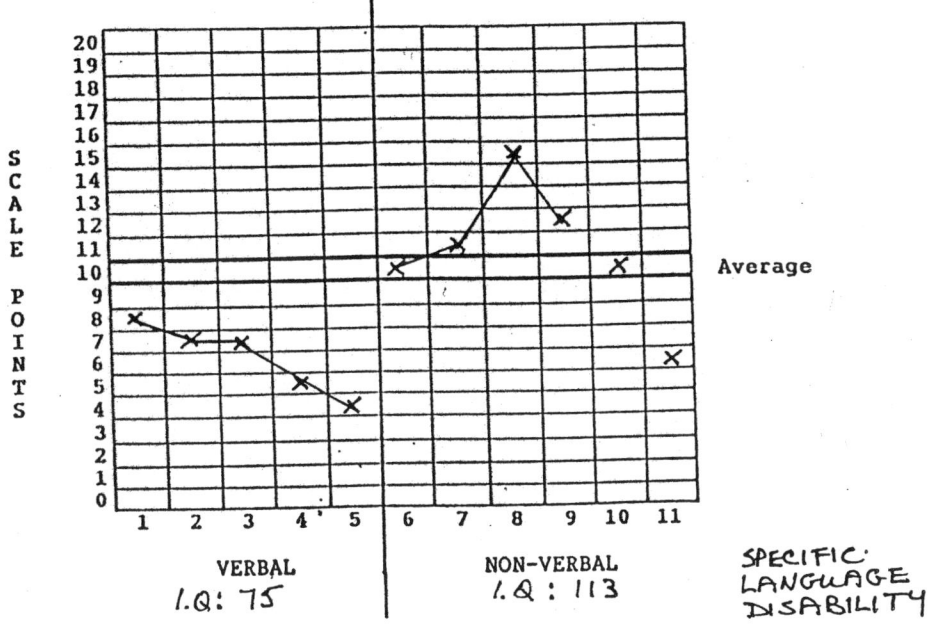

VERBAL

I.Q: 75

NON-VERBAL

I.Q : 113

SPECIFIC
LANGUAGE
DISABILITY

KEY:

1. Vocabulary
2. Comprehension
3. Similarities
4. Number Problems

5. Story Memory
6. Pattern Completion
7. Blocks
8. Missing Parts

9. Form Board
10. Memory for Digits
11. Coding

Figure 5: *A graph of an I.Q. assessment of a boy with a specific language disability.*

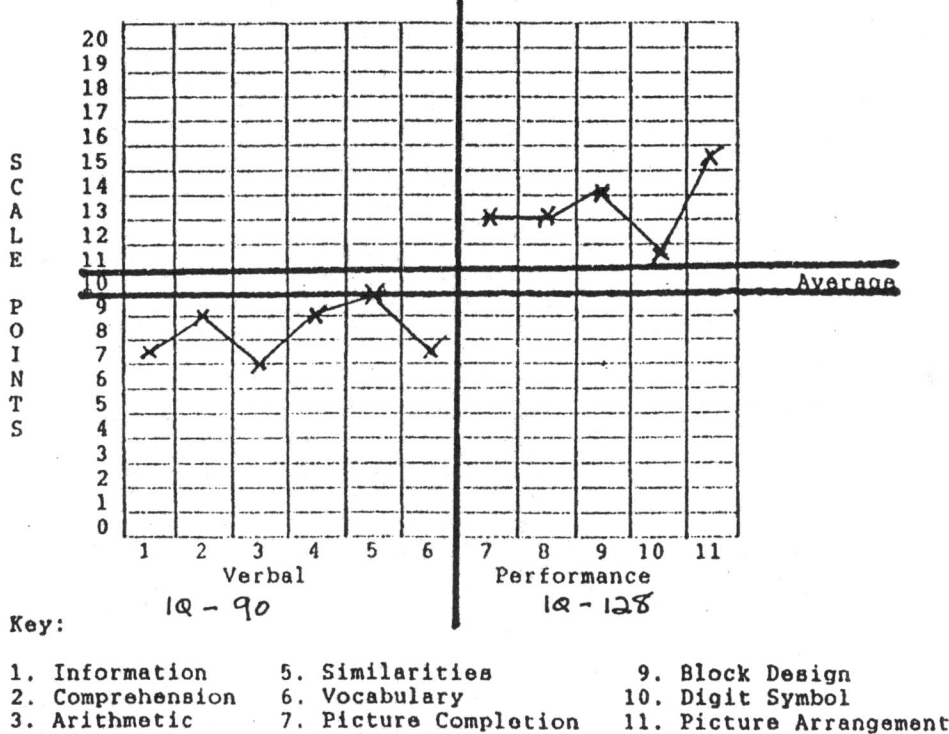

Figure 6: *A graph of an adult visual learner.*

HOME TRAITS

❑ Because of a selective lack of attention he ignores verbal instructions, particularly for mundane tasks such as going to bath. He will, how ever, respond very quickly if a sweet paper is rustled in the next room.

❑ He is slow to respond because of poor verbal processing.

❑ Many visual learners are left handed and if right handed, show left handed tendencies, sometimes working from right to left in drawing or colouring, or, holding a knife and fork in the opposite hands.

❑ In reporting events of the day he is muddled. When he dresses himself he is likely to put his shoes on before his trousers.

30

Figure 7: *Which go on first, my shoes or my socks?*

❏ He sees the day as a whole and has no sense of time. A comment heard commonly in many homes is, "What's the difference if I do it now or later?".

❏ He is imaginative and enjoys fantasy games. Parents will often say that he is able to amuse himself.

❏ He avoids doing his homework and will try to negotiate alternative times for doing it, which is a ploy to "put it off". A common avoidance tactic is to leave his books at home or at school and clashes with mother over doing homework occur frequently.

❏ He is a reluctant reader who does not listen to what he is reading and is slow to comprehend. Word recognition may be good but reading lacks flow and fluency.

❏ Parents are often surprised when their grade one child is reported by his teacher to be experiencing difficulties in the classroom, when he had a very positive pre-school history. This occurs because pre-school is a right brain environment and the formal school situation requires application of left brain skills.

❏ He prefers construction toys, Lego and board or card games, rather than those which involve listening or the use of language.

- Speech development may be delayed, with articulation errors occuring, for example, he may say, "lellow" for *yellow*, or "wabbit" for *rabbit* and "free" for *three*. Incorrect sequencing in expressive language occurs, such as saying, *melonade* for *lemonade*, *aminal* for *animal.*
- Speech development may be adequate for his chronological age but not in keeping with his physical development, which is often more advanced.
- He is an outdoor child who enjoys sport but may prefer non-competitive activities such as, swimming and tennis, rather than contact sports, such as rugby.
- He may resort to non-verbal communication, such as pulling faces.
- He tends to exaggerate when re-telling events, particularly those in which he has been involved.
- When talking, he has difficulty expressing himself and may resort to speaking in phrases or using gestures.
- He enjoys television and often turns up the sound volume very high.
- He may have a word finding difficulty where he refers to "stuff", or describes the object because he forgets the noun, for example he forgets the word "rake" and says, "I know it, it's the thing you use to sweep up the leaves with". Despite good hearing he will often say "What", "pardon", or "huh".
- Events from the past are remembered easily but he is unable to recall symbolic representations such as names, letters or numbers.

BEHAVIOURAL TRAITS
- He is a non-conformist, stubborn and selfwilled, often trying to manipulate situations to his own advantage.
- He is very sensitive, resorting to tears for no rhyme or reason.
- He is a poor mixer and often causes problems when playing with other children, because he does not understand the rules of the game.
- He is not competitive and will start an activity with enthusiasm, but does not follow through, for example, he will initiate going to karate or soccer and after a few sessions does not want to go any more.

The Adult Visual Learner

Since right brain dominance is organic and a matter of brain organisation, characteristics persist into adulthood, although there are some who have by then overcome many of their problems or developed compensatory skills.

Examples: Tom, aged 53, still has sequencing problems. He says *dymanic* for dynamic and when writing his name and telephone numbers, he confuses the order of the letters and numbers.

Hazell, who designed the cover of this book, has not overcome her language problems but has developed excellent artistic and visuo-spatial skills. She tells how she "beamed out" in high school, drawing strawberries with legs, in running shoes, in her biology lesson when her teacher talked about propagation by runners.

Figure 8: *Visual learners interpretation of "Propagation by runners".*

She and many other visual learners, who, although able to drive well, could not pass their written driving tests and required special dispensation to do the test orally.

Adult visual learners often acquire a liking for reading but prefer factual, non fiction books, or thrillers, where details can be visualised. However, because they like to see things as a whole, they will often read the end first. They usually become organised in adulthood, but they often still have untidy desks and drawers and muddled verbal expression.

SCREENING TESTS TO IDENTIFY RIGHT BRAIN DOMINANT VISUAL LEARNERS

For those seeking more substantial evidence than the characteristics listed above, to identify the right brain dominant visual learner, some brief screening techniques are suggested. It should be remembered that these are not tests. The purpose of the screening is to give an indication of the child's hemispheric preference for learning, and to make it easier to develop appropriate teaching strategies to help him cope more effectively.

The interpretations given for the five screening methods selected are derived from the author's clinical experience over the last 10 years, with several hundred children between the ages of five to nine years. The interpretations are not absolute, nor have they been subjected to research to validate them.

The five screening methods to indicate hemispheric dominance are:

❏ Bannatyne Simultaneous Writing Test.

❏ Automatic Unlearned Responses.

❏ Timed Hammering Sample.

❏ Muscle Testing.

❏ Eye Movements.

Bannatyne Simultaneous Writing Test

Purpose

To assess the dominance of one hemisphere of the brain, usually the left, verbal over the other, usually the right, spatial.

When mirror images, reversals of numbers and letters are produced by a young child, some authorities, for example, Bannatyne, ascribe the phenomenon to the brain being unlateralised in terms of the right hemisphere being suppressed by the left.

Instructions

Prepare a blank sheet of A4 paper by ruling a line down the centre, making two columns and marking them Left and Right. Then give the child two sharp pencils and tell him to write the numbers from 1 to 10 underneath each other, using both hands simultaneously, and working as quickly as possible. The results are invalid if he is allowed to work slowly and stop to think before responding.

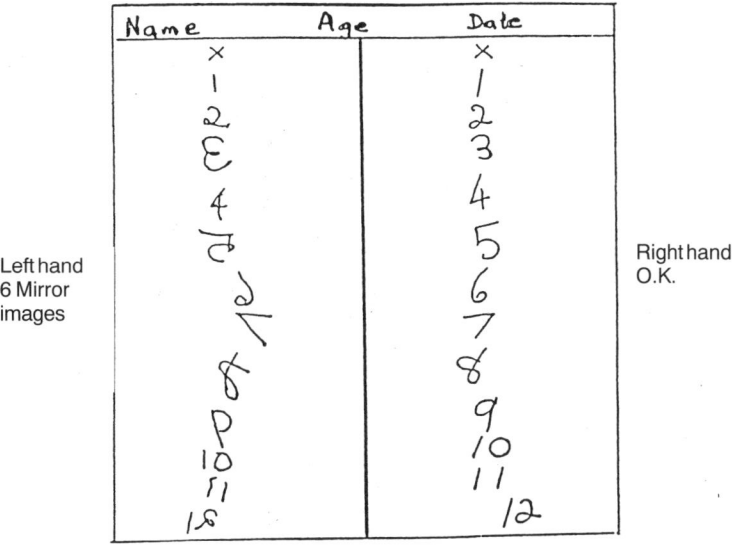

Left hand
6 Mirror
images

Right hand
O.K.

Figure 9: *A visual learners response on the Bannatyne Simultaneous Writing Test.*

Interpretation

The left-brain right-handed and under eight-year-old produces no mirror images with his dominant hand, and up to three mirror images with the non-dominant hand. This is within normal limits, although slightly immature. The response is the same in the right-brain left-hander.

The right-brain right-hander, however, often mirror images all the numbers with his left hand and none with his right. A severe lateralisation problem and maturational lag is indicated if several numbers are mirror imaged with both hands.

In rare instances where mirror images are produced with the dominant hand only, incorrect handedness may be suspected.

Caution

Do not change a child's hand dominance on the basis of this test alone.

It is also known that most children overcome their tendency to mirror image and reverse when the brain becomes more lateralised for language, and this accounts for young children who tend to produce mirror images and reversals, also showing immaturity in their language development.

Automatic Unlearned Responses

Purpose

To determine which hemisphere is dominant by checking responses when doing activities which are not learned responses, like writing. Take into account that the validity of these checks is increased if the observations are made three to four times and preferably on different days.

Thumb-finger circles

Ask the child to form a circle with his thumb and fore-finger and then successive circles with the other three fingers. Observe which hand is used as this is the one item which clearly determines hand dominance, because the child will always use his dominant hand.

Clapping hands

Ask the child to clap hands. The uppermost hand will usually be the dominant one.

Clasping hands

Ask the child to clasp his hands together tightly, with his fingers interlaced. The thumb that lies uppermost usually indicates the dominant hand.

Extending arms

Ask the child to close his eyes and extend his arms fully, then quickly place one arm over the top of the other. The uppermost arm is usually the dominant one.

Folding arms

Ask the child to fold his arms. The right hander will tend to place his right hand on top of his upper left arm and tuck the left hand under the right arm. These positions are reversed in the left hander. When neither hand is tucked in, the child may be ambi-dextrous.

Winding string

Ask the child to wind a length of string onto an empty reel, the dominant hand is usually the one that moves.

36

Tearing paper

Ask the child to pick up a piece of paper and tear it in half. The usual response is to pull towards the body with the dominant hand.

Interpretation

When hand and brain dominance are firmly established, there is good bilateral integration, where the side opposite the dominant hemisphere is used most of the time and is also stronger.

The right-brain right-hander and some lefthanders tend to have many more ambi-dextrous responses on these checks than the left-brain right-handers. One of the authors uses four of the checks mentioned here and frequently observes two left and two right sided responses in the right-brain right-handers.

Timed Hammering Sample

This screening procedure used by some occupational therapists was first described by Barbara Knickerbocker, an occupational therapist, in her book entitled, "An Holistic Approach to the Treatment of Learning Disorders"

Purpose

To determine hand preference and brain dominance by comparing the samples of each hand, using the Timed Hammering Sample.

Instructions

A carbon sheet is placed between two sheets of A4 paper which have a 10 cm circle drawn in the centre of the each page, secured onto a clip-board.

The child is given a small hammer and is told to strike hard and fast, staying in the centre of the circle and continuing until told to stop. The time allowed is 30 seconds and the number of strikes must be counted, preferably using a counter. Repeat the procedure with the other hand and record the number of strikes (see Appendix, page 153).

Observations include recording which hand was used first, comparing the quality of fine motor control of his two hands, based on the density, clustering and dispersion of strikes reflected on the carbon copy.

Figure 10: *The left brain, right hander's response.*

Figure 11: *The right brain, right hander's response (the visual learner).*

Interpretation

The usual pattern is for the child to strike approximately 10 to 15 times more frequently with the preferred hand, with better clustering and density.

The trend with the right-brain right-hander is to produce either the same number of strikes with both hands, or between two to four more with the preferred hand. Even if he has the same number of strikes with

38

each hand, he will show his preference by using his dominant hand first and produce a sample with the strikes clustered centrally, as opposed to the non-dominant hand, where the strikes are often widely dispersed. Children who produce many more strikes with the non-dominant hand may be presenting with mixed dominance.

MUSCLE TESTING

Purpose

To test the relative strength of the arm muscles and to determine hemispheric preference, as the strong side is usually dominant.

Instructions

With the child standing comfortably, feet slightly apart and facing you, ask him to raise one arm straight out from his shoulder at a 90 degree angle. Then put your hand on his opposite shoulder and place two fingers of your other hand on the wrist of his extended arm whilst saying, "I am going to push your arm down, I want you to stop me from pushing it down. You must not push up but just hold tight". Repeat the procedure with the other arm, after observing for muscle locking, or a definite demonstration of strength, record which side is strongest.

Weakness reflects reduced muscle tone and is commonly observed in right-brain visual learners, often accounting for a poor sitting posture when working at his desk. When both sides are strong the child is able to use both hemispheres selectively in relation to the task.

Mixed dominance is suspected when it is difficult to detect a strong side but it could also reflect a tendency to alternate from one hemisphere to the other. Such children present as confused, dis-organised learners.

EYE MOVEMENTS

Purpose

To determine hemispheric dominance by observing eye movements, as research studies have shown that if one hemisphere is stimulated, the eyes will turn towards the opposite side of the body.

Instructions

With the child facing you, make eye contact and present verbal stimuli appropriate for activating either a left or right hemisphere response. Also present stimuli that are age appropriate. Here are some examples:

Questions to elicit right brain responses:

- ❑ "What did you eat for breakfast?"
- ❑ "What does the word 'sad' mean?"
- ❑ "What is your favourite colour?"

Questions to elicit left brain responses:

- ❑ "How do you spell your name?"
- ❑ "Where is the stove in your kitchen?"
- ❑ "How much is 7 plus 4?"

In her book, Unicorns Are Real, Barbara Meister-Vitale says the following,

"Observations of eye movements can be used to identify the child's primary learning modality. Since the auditory centre is in the left hemisphere, movement of the eyes to the right suggests an auditory learner. Eye movements to the left suggests that the child is a visual learner and right brained. Some children move their eyes towards the top of their head rather than right or left. These children seem to be haptic learners and often have no hemispheric preference. These children learn through body movement and touch. They are the children who learn through hands on experience". (Haptic means learning by touch). Additional screening techniques described include:

Checking hand position when writing, the right-brain right-hander sometimes adopts a 'hooked' hand position

Hooked Right

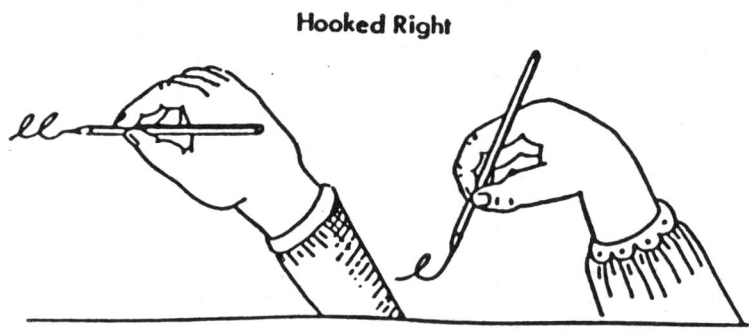

Figure 12: *Hand positions adopted by some visual learners.*

Observing body symmetry, where the side of the body that is larger and fuller, is usually opposite the dominant hemisphere.

Finally, there is open ended questioning where interpretation of the child's response makes it possible to determine both hemispheric dominance and preferred learning style (visual, auditory or haptic).

In conclusion, it should be evident from the foregoing that if the child's learning style has been determined, it becomes much easier for his parents and his teacher to provide the kind of assistance that will ensure that he profits from his learning experiences.

PART 2

HOW DO WE HELP THIS CHILD?

CHAPTER **4**

Behavioural Management

WHEN a parent says to us, "If I apply these behavioural manage ment techniques that you advocate, will my children *always* respond?".

Our reply is, "Not necessarily, as children are not robots!" We are also not suggesting ways to manipulate your children to react in a predictable way. On the contrary, our message is to be sensitive to their needs by helping them to use their initiative, act intelligently, be responsible and above all to be good listeners.

The parents' ultimate goal should be to create an emotional climate that encourages their children to co-operate because they care about themselves. Children who have positive self images and self respect are the ones most likely to show respect towards others, which carries over into adulthood.

REASONS FOR GOOD BEHAVIOUR

Before any child can cope successfully with a teaching programme, it is essential that he is in control of his own behaviour. In handling the visual learner it is necessary to remember that he needs the security of consistent discipline, which is best achieved in a structured and organised environment.

This principle applies to all children but is more relevant for the visual learner who is slow to process language and does not listen well.

He tends to respond very slowly to social situations, becomes confused and reacts immaturely, with frustration, aggression, hyperactivity or tears. He needs to have limits set for him and models of behaviour that he can follow.

Do not attempt to change a visual learner into an auditory learner. Right brain dominance is a matter of brain organisation like left handedness. One should not encourage a left hander to become right handed. For example, Steve, who went to school in Europe, was left handed and when he broke his left arm at nine years of age, he was made to use his right hand, which he then continued to do. Now a young adult in South Africa, he has decided to write left handed again and has had no difficulty in doing so. It has, in fact, made it easier for him to study in English, a new language for him, by freeing his left brain to concentrate on language while the right brain took over it's natural control of the left hand.

DISCIPLINE

There should be a few sets of rules, but not too many, so as not to confuse the child. He should know which behaviour is, or is not, acceptable. Distinguish between unacceptable and inappropriate be-

LA PASTAAAA !

Figure 1: *"No singing at the supper table please!"*

haviour. The former should not be tolerated under any circumstances and requires effective consequences to be imposed immediately, to prevent re-occurence. The latter implies that the behaviour can be accepted, but only at certain times and in specified places.

For example, shouting is unacceptable, singing is appropriate, provided it occurs in the church, in the bath, in the singing lessons, etc. It should not be allowed at the dinner table or in the class-room.

The following is an example of inappropriate behaviour from a visual learner which interfered with her performance level in the classroom. The whole class was told by the teacher to write a story of at least one page in length, which also had a title. Jenny started to write the title of her story and, taking her time, formed the letters in such a way that they looked pretty and flowery. She then picked up her crayons and started to colour in the various letters of the title. By the time that some members of the class had already completed their stories, Jenny had not yet

Figure 2: *Jenny decorating the title of her story*

46

started writing hers. In such a case it is essential that the teacher makes it clear that decorating letters is not bad behaviour but doing it in the class room, when she should be writing her story, makes it bad behaviour.

By imposing outside limits the child can learn self-discipline. He should be given the opportunity to express his feelings verbally but his behaviour should be controlled so that he does not become violent or destructive.

Ginott describes permissiveness as "an attitude of accepting imaginary and symbolic behaviour". Some examples are the childishness of getting dirty, running instead of walking, climbing trees and pulling faces in a mirror.

Destructive behaviour is not acceptable and being too permissive allows undesirable acts. Limits should be clearly stated, for example, "You may not write on walls but you may write on sheets of paper".

Allow active behaviour and emotional outlet, for example, running around, hitting a tennis ball against the wall or punching a punch-bag. Instructions must be stated in simple language with no threat or anger in one's tone of voice. Explanations should be brief and explicit, for example, "Windows must not be broken".

Children become anxious when they have exceeded the limits and threats increase their anxiety and bring fear of retaliation. Mutual respect between parents and children should be maintained and the child must not be demeaned as a person.

Models

Figure 3: *"If possible, ignore bad behaviour"*

Parents are models for behaviour and should consistently set a good example. "Do as I say and not as I do" confuses the child. Little white lies, impoliteness and dishonesty on the part of adults, whom the child respects, may be construed as acceptable behaviour. Children identify with parents and adopt their values to set their own standards.

Punishment

It is often necessary to punish, but in excess it loses efficacy. Often an explanation of the error of his ways is sufficient, although the child forgets and his good intentions may be short-lived. Hidings work temporarily and teach aggression, as well as relieving the child's guilt, so that misbehaviour can be repeated.

Time out (where the child is punished by being sent to a quiet spot on his own for a short period to cool off) and behaviour modification (where techniques are devised to alter the child's behaviour to be more in keeping with accepted norms) work for some children but most of them have poor self images. Positive reinforcement in the form of stars for younger children, and praise for good behaviour is usually more effective. One may have to search hard for something to praise and it is difficult to ignore negative or attention seeking behaviour. In the long run, however, it pays off.

Rewards for good behaviour may take the form of words of gratitude, hugs or privileges, and need not necessarily be material like money or gifts. For example, to stay up ten minutes later to see something special on television, or to accompany parents on a outing.

Parental feelings

It is not easy to be a parent, particularly when the child has a problem. One feels anger or despair and one should not deny one's feelings. Just as a child benefits from physical activities to disperse his frustration or anger, so will the parents sometimes feel better after a brisk walk, or getting away on their own for a short while.

One can say to the child, "That is making me cross". Always make it clear that it is the *behaviour* and *not your child* that you dislike. Do not be afraid to say, "How would you feel if you were me?", or, "What would you say to your child?"

Children often come home from school feeling upset after a frustrating day, so try to be relaxed and hear them out. It is important to listen. Your responses may be non-committal, such as, "That made you feel bad, I'm so sorry about it". This is as comforting as offering solutions which you may not have, and allows him to get his feelings off his chest.

It does mother good to take off an hour or two occasionally of a morning to go shopping, or have tea with a friend.

For working parents it is the *quality* of time you give your child that makes an impact. Fifteen minutes of your individual attention is more valuable than a whole day of being impatient, brushing him off with, "I'm busy", or responding with, "Mmm" and not listening. This is particularly so for fathers, who would do better to discuss matters interesting to the child, than to ask, "What did you do in school today?".

Children must respect parents' needs and allow them to relax and unwind after work, before demanding their attention. Families benefit from togetherness with meals, with each member of the family having a chance to express themselves. By asking the child what he thinks, he is encouraged to think for himself, to listen, participate in discussions and to feel accepted and important.

Responsibility

Responsibility helps the child to think and grow as a person and improve his self image. Ginott says that, "A good self image cannot be imposed but it grows from within, fed by values absorbed at home and in the community. It is based on respect for life, liberty and the pursuit of happiness".

Responsibility is acquired with age and experience and children should be allowed choices in matters affecting them from an early age, set by parental limits. For example, allow him to choose his own clothes or food, from a selection chosen by the parents. Give pocket money and make him responsible for it. This teaches him to budget for his own needs. Remember, pocket money should not be a reward for chores or good behaviour.

Conversing with the Visual Learner

All children need to be talked to right from the cradle, even before they have a good understanding of the spoken word. With the visual learner one's language should be descriptive, making use of movement and pictures wherever possible. Use social phrases like, "please" and "thank-you", for them to learn to be polite to others. This makes them more acceptable socially, even when they are unable to express themselves easily.

At School

Allowances should be made for visual learners whose language skills are immature. They are slower to comprehend than many of their peers, disorganised in verbal and written expression and do not listen well. The fact that they are very bright in other respects is not usually seen in the language orientated classroom and they do not have the opportunity to prove themselves. They either blend quietly into the back-ground, are disruptive or become the class clown. They may read well mechanically, without comprehension and under pressure of tests they go to pieces.

Figure 4: *Test pressure*

They need to be treated with some tolerance on the part of the teacher, who may need to repeat instructions, preferably individually in simple language. It should be accepted that they cannot learn easily by listening or reading notes and should be encouraged to use their right brain visual skills.

Spelling dispensation should be given and labelled diagrams should be accepted in place of written work if possible. A good rapport with the teacher makes for a much better self image and helps to maintain motivation.

Remedial tuition should involve language development which falls into the realm of the speech therapist, viz, vocabulary, comprehension, verbal expression, auditory and listening skills.

Homework

Homework can become a painful issue and a source of friction. It also causes jealousy and feelings of inferiority when a sibling works faster. It is therefore advisable to let the child do his homework on his own, without a sibling helping, or peeping over his shoulder.

If the parent understands the problem and can help him use visual graphic techniques to study without clashing with him, her assistance would be invaluable. If not, it is better to leave him to his own devices for a specified time, then sign the homework book to indicate that he has tried.

He should not receive too much homework as he may not be able to complete the assignment successfully. He will achieve no more by sitting for an hour, than for fifteen minutes, if he cannot read, comprehend or do maths. Limit the time for homework, or break the times up into shorter periods. Remember that his concentration span is limited.

Figure 5: *"I can't cope with all this homework!"*

The visual learner is the one who often comes home from school tired, frustrated and unmotivated, because of the amount of effort that has been put in trying to grasp what does not come easily to him in the classroom.

It is wise to allow him some opportunity to expend physical energy, and have a bite to eat before sitting down to his homework. It is always advisable to complete homework before the evening meal, in order to allow relaxed family time afterwards.

Bedtime

Children are often apprehensive about the school day to come and are unwilling to go to sleep. Sleep should be preceded by a quiet, warm, loving period. One parent should sit beside the bed and read a story, preferably with a happy ending. Stories which are easily visualised are more acceptable. There should be no anger, recrimination or punishment so that the child retires with love, acceptance and happiness.

BEDTIME

Figure 6: *"I wish I could stay at home tomorrow"*

Is the visual learner a victim of the educational system?

Being a visual learner is not the problem. It is an unaccomodating educational system that creates the problem. There is no reason why the visual learner, or right brain adult should not find a comfortable niche for himself in this world and make a success of his life.

The child should not be labelled as being learning disabled, because if the educational system catered for the visual learner, there would not be a problem.

It is also important not to say to the child, "You are right-brain domi-nant", because he may think that there is something wrong with him. It is sufficient to say, "You are a visual learner, it's a different way but not an inferior way to learn and there are many other visual learners, although many of them have not been identified"

However, as he passes through the school system his ego takes a battering and he may no longer have a positive self image. He *knows* that he is not coping. He feels more comfortable when he is told that he does have a problem, but that many other people in the adult world also had learning problems, for example, Einstein, Churchill, Tony Factor and Arthur Bleksley. The latter was told by his class teacher that her gardener had far more intelligence than he had and that it was unlikely that he would ever matriculate. The final outcome was that Arthur Bleksley became one of the world's greatest astrono-mers and a scientist who was a respected professor at the University of The Witwatersrand.

Point out to him that although these people had problems like his, they were nonetheless intelligent, and became examples to others.

He is then comforted in the knowledge that he is not alone and is handicapped by the system. It is also important to ensure that this does not tempt him to sit back and blame the system. He has to realise that *he can help himself* and should do so. This can be done by praise for what he does well, not necessarily school related. Encourage his hobbies and in-terests, ensuring that he is loved and accepted for who he is.

The visual learner is confused by his inability to achieve well and be-lieves that he is stupid. He feels better about himself when he realises why certain subjects are more difficult for him than for his peers. It is better to face the problem than to hide it. He is then able to understand why, for example, he can do geometry and not algebra, and feel moti-vated to try instead of giving up. A learning disability cannot be ignored or swept under the carpet, nor should it be kept from the school after an assessment has been done. It must come out into the open and be dealt with. The problem should be tackled on two fronts, by remediating the weak areas and by building up his strengths to compensate.

In the case of the visual learner this means therapy to develop better language and auditory skills whilst simultaneously teaching visual study techniques. As visual learning often has a genetic component the child feels less isolated in the family if he knows that he shares his problem with a parent, sibling, or other relation.

The issue is a family affair and the child cannot be left to bear his problem alone. Siblings should be encouraged to accept that visual learners are as clever as they are but in a different way and competition should be avoided by the cultivation of different hobbies and interests, this being particularly important if the children are close in age, or of the same sex. For example, there was a mother who had three little daughters aged 6, 7 and 9. She took them to ballet regularly, disregarding the fact that the seven year old hated going. From her point of view it was easier to take all three to the same place.

Some points to remember

Do not let negative aspects overshadow his life. Allow the child to participate in sport. Physical exercise is good for stress release, improves concentration and is therapeutic.

One achieves nothing by saying that because he is not doing well at school, he must stay at home and read. Let him participate in pleasures close to his heart and let there be times when he runs around with no purpose other than to let off steam, or do nothing.

Sport at which he may often excel should not be dropped in order that he spend more time doing homework. It is necessary for him and his peers to know that there are areas where he can achieve successfully, for example, karate and ball skills.

Look for hobbies and interests, encourage music, drawing and participation in creative activities such as making models, pottery or wood carving, board or card games, or chess. Girls may enjoy knitting, sewing, baking and cooking. Children may also enjoy having their own gardens, but keep this patch small to begin with, so that they can cope successfully.

Pets provide an emotional and caring relationship for any child and he should be encouraged to care for his pets.

A punch bag is an excellent outlet for aggression and anger and could be hung in an accessible place, out of the way, where he can be alone to vent his frustrations.

With a small child, let him sit next to you and look at the pictures while you are reading to him, even if he is able to read for himself. When he has gone beyond stories, read history or other subjects to improve his knowledge, allowing him the time to visualise the subject matter.

Do not exert pressure for high marks. Accept that he has done his best. Do not push him to study, leave this responsibility to him and the school, otherwise he could become resistant. Remember, you can only lead a horse to the water, not make him drink. For example, do not say, "You did well but if you tried harder you could do better". The moment you say, "but", the second statement negates the first.

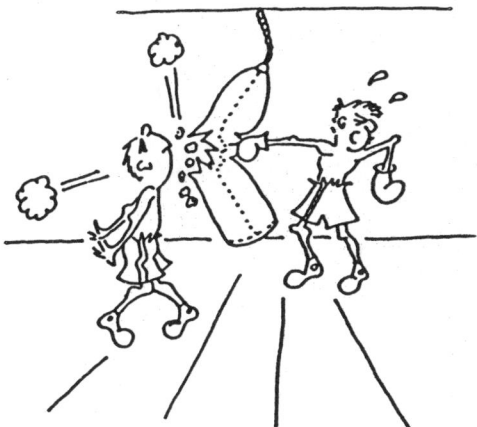

Figure 7: *"This makes me feel so much better"*

Encourage conversation, within acceptable limits, allow gestures and facial expression to help him express himself, even though he may fumble for words. Do not become impatient and do not do his talking for him.

Allow him to watch television as long as it is not for too long, not violent, and preferably not soap operas. There are worth-while programmes that should be encouraged. Help him to select appropriate programmes.

Do not feel desperate and do not avoid professional help. There are facilities for counselling for parents and children, for family therapy, play therapy, speech therapy, remedial teaching, occupational therapy and extra lessons.

When in doubt, or when you have an inkling that something is amiss, follow it up by discussing it with the school and arranging for an appropri-

Figure 8: *"Reading together is fun"*

55

ate assessment of his learning or emotional status.

The visual learner cannot be detected easily in the classroom and is often not referred for an assessment. Parents should not hesitate to follow their own intuition and should remember that they owe it to their child to ensure that he derives maximum benefit from his education.

Routinely check your child's vision, preferably with a paediatric optometrist because good vision is a pre-requisite for visual learning. The paediatric optometrist assesses the visual functions for learning, namely, eye coordination, scanning, occular motor control, depth perception, accomodation and colour blindness.

These aspects are important in the classroom because if there is visual stress, the child tires, thus accentuating the problem and making it harder for him to concentrate.

Hearing should be assessed, preferably by an audiologist at the pre school stage, to ascertain whether or not there is a physiological cause for poor listening. The visual learner does not listen well, he has a selective lack of attention.

What should parents do?

Parental anxiety is not allayed by being told that "He will grow out of it", "He is lazy", "Naughty", or, "You are being over-anxious", "You are expecting too much from him", or "He is slow or backward or dyslexic".

Parents are entitled to make an appointment with the school psychologist at the local Educational Psychological Support Services, to go to a private clinic, or seek the help of a psychologist of their choice. The latter should be experienced in working with children with learning difficulties, who will refer a primarily emotional problem to a clinical specialist, usually a colleague, who will work with the family.

One should aim at improving weak areas and simultaneously teach compensatory skills. Conventional remedial methods, using phonics alone, are not successful without drawing on visual memory. For example, pictures, flash cards and bringing in rhymes and tunes to help memorise spellings or tables.

When talking to him, make eye contact and keep instructions short and simple (KISS principle)

Set aside a time to listen to your child. Be patient and recognise him as a person in his own right, who needs praise and encouragement.

Remember, teachers are for teaching and parents are for parenting. A teacher should change her role to that of parent when she goes home to her family.

Encourage your child to do his homework independently and sign his homework notebook after a specific time.

Figure 9. *Do not do his homework for him*

There are undoubtedly many parents who recognise some of the suggestions, as they are already making use of them and hopefully there are many more parents who will be motivated to apply some of the principles suggested and derive the benefits, not only for themselves, but for their whole family and particularly for the visual learner.

CHAPTER 5

Strategies to develop basic skills for learning

IT IS universally accepted that the child who has well developed basic skills for learning is better equipped to cope with the demands of formal schooling. The visual learner is, however, at a disadvantage when exposed to opportunities to develop these basic skills.

He is usually too busy playing with his Lego or construction toys, watching television or running around outside, to be become involved and profit from the more organised, disciplined and sometimes repetitive kinds of activities such as colouring, cutting, pasting and drawing. Consequently he jeopardises his own chances of becoming proficient in his performance of tasks in these areas.

Successful learning is dependent on well developed skills in five major areas, namely;

❑ Language and related skills
❑ Sensory motor skills
❑ Dominance, directional and left-right concepts
❑ Visual perception and visual memory
❑ Auditory perception and auditory memory

Sub-skills in the language area include speech, comprehension, vocabulary and creative writing.

Sub-skills in the sensory motor area are, body image, gross motor skills, eye-hand coordination and fine motor control.

Sub-skills in the dominance area include directional and left-right concepts, body-space integration, a sound knowledge of left and right as they relate to the body, as well as mastering the understanding of the directional orientation of letters and numbers.

Sub-skills in the visual perceptual area are, discrimination, sequential memory, spatial relationships, form constancy, figure-ground and closure.

Sub-skills in the auditory area include listening, discrimination, figure-ground perception, sequential memory and closure.

The discussion of basic skills development will be confined to three contentious issues that have been selected on the basis of being the concerns expressed most frequently by parents and teachers.

These are:

❑ Poor listening skills.
❑ Poor co-ordination, with specific difficulty regarding the use of scissors.
❑ Finally, to produce mirror images, reversals and incorrect sequencing of letters and numbers in their written work.

In the visual learner, visual perceptual skills are usually well developed and will consequently not be given much attention in this guide. It should however be emphasised that parents and teachers should take advantage of his strengths, capitalising on them, to help him have success experiences which will contribute towards developing and maintaining a positive self image and also improve his level of confidence.

In addition to the suggestions that follow, it is very helpful when working with pre-school children, to also make use of the "Accelerate Programme", which is a pre-school enrichment programme for parents, designed by an occupational therapist and a speech therapist. Consisting of six books, the programme provides daily activities, check-lists and guidelines for developing skills in the following areas,

❑ Body-Image
❑ Movement Skills
❑ Language Skills
❑ Body-Space Integration
❑ Visual Perceptual Processing
❑ Auditory Perceptual Processing.

For more details of these programmes see Appendix, page 144.

House of learning

Integrated learning					
Self study					
Maths (Arithmetic)					
Writing					
Reading					
Body image	Movement skills	Language skills	Body space integration	Visual perception	Auditory perceptions

Figure 1: *House of Learning*

59

LISTENING SKILLS

Research has shown that children respond better to softer voices. If you are inclined to speak loudly, try whispering and the response will surprise you.

Figure 2: *Children "Switch off" to loud voices*

There is a need to make a distinction between commands and requests. While the term 'command' may sound harsh, it really only means that compliance is expected. A request implies that the child has a choice. Have you not heard fathers say, "My wife tells our son to go and bath and I know from her tone of voice that he is doing her a favour" and there won't be any consequences for noncompliance.

Listening behaviour comprises two elements, verbal and non-verbal. The non-verbal side involves relaxed posture, eye contact, gestures, nodding and facial expressions. Verbal behaviour includes simple statements such as, uh huh, or yes, or joining in his story, or paraphrasing to let him know that you are listening to him.

Figure 3: *Listen to him and he will listen to you*

Remember that closed questions produce a yes or no response and discourage conversation, whilst open ended questions give freedom to steer the discussion into the area of his choice, for example, an open question would be; "What did you do at school today?", whereas a closed question could be, "Did you fail your test today?".

Suggestions to improve his listening
- ❑ Use his name to attract his attention.
- ❑ Maintain eye contact.
- ❑ Give instructions once only.
- ❑ When complex instructions have been given, aid his memory by asking him to repeat the instruction before making a response.
- ❑ Be a good listener yourself.
- ❑ In some situations expect him to remain seated, for example, when you are reading a story to him.
- ❑ Play listening games, for example, whispering telephone.
- ❑ Make use of a tape recorder which accepts a head-phone.
- ❑ Encourage the learning of rhymes and simple poems.
- ❑ Give him practice in re-telling a story.
- ❑ Do not lose the opportunity to praise him for being a good listener.

CO-ORDINATION
Using a pair of scissors more efficiently

When doing cutting, pasting, colouring and drawing activities work at a desk or table, seat him on a comfortable chair, with his feet firmly on the floor. His table should also be at the correct height for him to work easily and he should be encouraged to plan ahead, coming to the table prepared with his books, crayons, pencil, and a pair of scissors. He must be discouraged from leaving the table until the activities that he has chosen to do have been completed.

It is vital for the remediator to remember that the visual learner does not respond well to verbal instructions and sometimes even has difficulty imitating from observations. He has to be shown by demonstration, which involves teaching him how to make the movements by directly instructing him through touch and physical participation.

For example, when learning to use a pair of scissors he begins with the teacher asking him to touch his thumb and fore-finger together several times. He holds neither the paper nor the scissors but concentrates on performing the opening and closing movements that simulate cutting.

His fingers may need to be guided, simultaneously saying, "open, shut, open, shut". He is then given a pair of scissors and is encouraged to repeat the same movements.

Be careful to explain how his fingers fit into the scissor handles. As he opens and closes his fingers, draw his attention to the blades, encouraging him to look at how they open and close.

As he moves his fingers it is important for him to see the entire operation before he begins to cut, as he will then only see the top blade and cannot easily perceive the total cutting movement.

When the opening and closing movements have been mastered, let him make short cuts along the paper's edge, whilst you hold the paper for him, to enable him to concentrate on the cutting movement. Use heavy paper at first as it easier to cut because there is less tension on the scissor blades.

Continue to hold the paper and ask him to make three or four cuts across the paper.

He has now learned the skills and needs encouragement to have repetitive practice, with no negative comments being made for poor performance and praise for good performance.

Figure 4: *Learning to use a pair of scissors*

It should be remembered that all activities designed to improve fine motor control and particularly paper and pencil tasks, need to be presented in a variety of ways, to maintain a sustained effort, as repetitive practice is the key to success.

Mirror images and reversals

Before considering the implications of poorly developed skills in the understanding of directional and left-right concepts, which lead to producing mirror images and reversals, there is a need to dispel some of the myths and evaluate some of the research on the topic.

Firstly, the concept of 'cerebral dominance' has limited validity amongst present day neurologists and has been supplemented in modern neurological theory by the concept of hemispheric specialisation.

The term **dominance** will nonetheless still be used in this guide when referring to a child's hand preference.

Some research has been done on four and five year old children which has shown that they can be taught left, right, up, down, top and bottom and learn to discriminate and to understand directionality, provided that they are given correct instruction.

The significance of these findings is that letter and number recognition is a learned, cognitive behaviour and is not a developmental perceptual skill. There is also considerable evidence to show that maturity levels do not affect reversal errors, that is, if a maturity level of six years is cited for reversals, then attempts to teach these skills to younger children should be unsuccessful and yet all the experimental evidence is to the contrary.

Many authorities, including Bannatyne (1972), Kirschner (1971) and Orton (1961), have speculated that the reversing of symbols is due to rivalry in hemispheric dominance.

The visual learner is more prone to produce mirror images and reversals because he has to suppress (switch off) his dominant hemisphere, which is more difficult than suppressing the non-dominant hemisphere, as it requires more neurological impulses to be activated. If the suppression does not occur, or is incomplete, mirror images are produced.

To avoid the tendency to reverse and mirror image, the child needs to be taught the importance of directionality as a distinguishing feature. The young child recognises forms and objects as identical, in spite of different orientation, that is, form constancy, but when confronted with letters and numbers, he finds that the form constancy rule no longer applies.

His past experience does not require that he regard spatial orientation as important because a chair is a chair in any position, and if his cat lies facing the door, it does not become a dog when it faces the opposite wall. However, when a 'b' is turned around, it suddenly becomes a 'd' and an 'f' facing the other way, is no longer called an 'f'.

The most beneficial teacher response to reversals, mirror imaging and sequencing errors, is to plan an instructional programme making use of the following guidelines

❑ Discrimination is the first task to teach, preferably before letter names.

❑ Matching letters with similar shapes is the first step.

❑ Focus attention on the direction of the letter or number as the critical feature. Overlaps may be used.

❑ In direct matching, where the sample letter is available for comparison and has been mastered, introduce the delayed matching task.

❑ He has to remember the directional orientation of a letter while looking for its match. He is required to remember the direction that it is facing as he cannot make a direct comparison.

❑ The best results are achieved through repetitive practice, using the same letter until it has been mastered.

❑ Letter names should only be taught after memory for the direction of the letter is accurate and automatic.

❑ A useful test to measure the normal-abnormal limits of visual receptive reversals in children between the ages of six to thirteen, is the Jordan Left-Right Reversals Test.

AN EFFECTIVE TECHNIQUE FOR THE TRAINING OF THE DIRECTIONAL ORIENTATION OF NUMBERS

Establish whether the child is familiar with the capital B, this being his first reference point. Ask him to print a B, then print it again, separating the vertical line on the left of the letter, producing a 1 and a 3. Say to him, "You can see that B breaks up into two numbers, a 1 and a 3".

Then tell him that 2 starts at the same point as the 3. Verbalise the movements, saying, "Start at the left, round to the right and back down to left and across to the right".

Learn the 7, which also starts on the left, like the 2 and the 3. Teach him to say the rhyme, "Across the top and down from heaven, that's the way to make a 7". Review and say, "From B comes 1, 2, 3 and 7.

Learn the 9, which differs only in one small part of it's construction. Say, "Moving to the left I make an oval, and down the line, that's the way to make a 9".

Learn the 4, which like 9, has it's vertical line to the right of the number. Say, "Down to the left and over to the right, then down once more, that's the way to make a 4".

Next comes 8. Say, "I make an S and then up straight, that's the way to make an 8".

Only 5 and 6 remain as potential sources of directional confusion. The second reference point is C. Say, "Like a C, I circle down and round to make a 6".

Finally, teach the mnemonic for 5, which says, "Short neck, body fat, number 5 wears a hat".

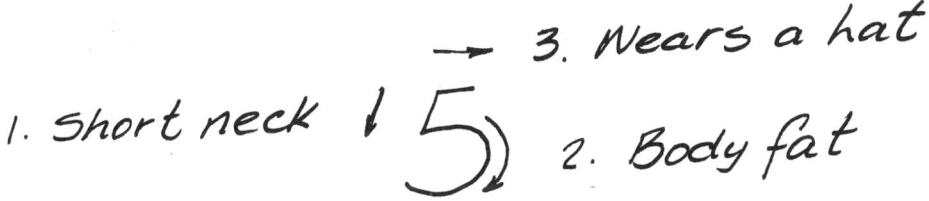

Figure 5: *A helpful mnemonic for learning to write a five*

When teaching the writing of numbers from 1 to 100, it is easier if they are aligned vertically, rather than horizontally, and becomes still easier if squared or graph paper is used.

Do not take it for granted that he knows or realises that once he is passed the teens, the first number in sequence is the one said first, such as, twenty five, sixty four, etc.

AN EFFECTIVE TECHNIQUE FOR REMEMBERING THE DIRECTIONAL ORIENTATION OF LETTERS

Various training suggestions have been described, with most using blue and red colour codes, b being for blue and left, and an explanation that the vertical line of the B is on the side closest to the margin; whilst d is for red and right, because d has it's vertical line on the right.

Figure 6 illustrates how Kenny, aged eight, who always mirror imaged his name, was shown how to write his name correctly.

A blue cardboard strip approximately 2 cm wide and 10 cm long was placed vertically against the margin of the writing page, with his name written vertically to the right side of the strip.

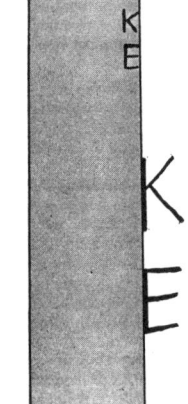

Figure 6: *Making the first stroke of 'K' and 'E' with a cardboard ruler*

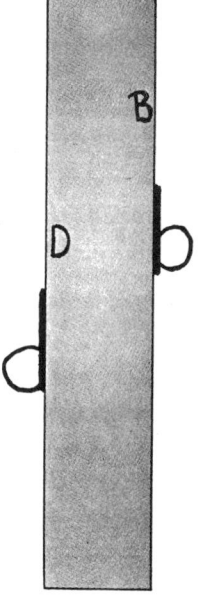

Figure 7: *Making the first stroke of 'b' and 'd' with a cardboard ruler*

He was then told to repeat the process for the capital K only, then the only way to complete his name was in the right direction. After practising this method ten times, he no longer needed the cardboard strip.

To help solve the b and d dilemma, he was given the cardboard strip with a capital B written at the top right and capital D in the middle left. Using the cardboard he was asked to write the words, bun, bat, ball, bee and boy, with the upright of each b against the cardboard strip. Then with the strip placed on the right he was asked to write d, and remove the strip, then complete the word, dog, replace the strip and again write the d, before completing the word doll, and likewise with the words, dig and dam.

He was then given the words, bad, bed, bid and bud to write, using the strip for each word. Finally, he wrote these words without the cardboard strip, introducing it only when errors occured. When his b and d confusion was overcome, other reversals such as p and q were elimated one at a time, using the same procedures.

Success, when applying this procedure, is more likely if one set of reversals is eliminated before teaching the second.

Teacher Instruction

The significance of the instructions that teachers give to children is illustrated by the following example.

Jane was referred for help because of her tendency to frequently mirror image her name when writing it. The assessment did not reveal any lags in the development of her skills and there was no accounting for her tendency to mirror image. The therapist visited the school and asked the teacher if she could be permitted to do a functional and task analysis, to determine the source of Jane's difficulty. It was discovered that there were no other mirror images or reversals in her books and the lack of consistency in her performance, where she only mirror imaged her name, was confusing.

Then, when the class were busy doing a drawing the teacher said, "There are only five minutes left, would everybody please clean up and remember to write your name in the lower right hand corner just like real artists do". To illustrate, she held up a piece of paper and indicated the lower right hand corner with her pencil. Jane picked up her pencil and carefully printed a J in the bottom right hand corner, then paused, seemed undecided and placed the a to the left of it. She completed her name in the familiar mirror image.

The therapist then asked her if she was aware of the way she had written her name on the piece of art work. "You mean it's backwards" she said, "I know that, it's because it won't fit the other way". This was pointed out to the teacher, who, on the next occasion changed her instruction to, "Please write your name anywhere along the bottom of the paper". Jane wrote her name correctly because with this instruction she was free to begin at any point and she elected to start quite far from the right hand corner to allow herself enough room for all the letters to be put in, in the proper sequence.

In this instance, Jane did not have a specific learning disability but was applying the teachers instructions correctly.

Additional suggestions

Daily practice on the arrow chart, where the concepts of left, right, up and down, are learned to the point where responses are quick, spontaneous and automatic, will contribute substantially to learning the directional orientation of letters and numbers.

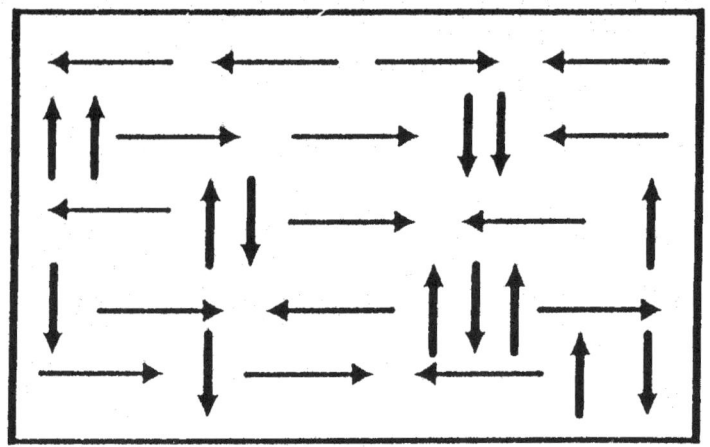

Figure 8: *The Arrow Chart*

If a child commences writing on the right hand side of his page, tell him to start on the left, or physically lift his hand to start on the left, because he will not then write to the left, off the page, and even if reversals and mirror images do still occur, there is still assurance that his movement is in the correct direction (to the right).

Children who are slow with their writing are often the ones who do not easily recall what letters look like and having a small card pasted on the top right hand corner of the desk, with all the alphabet letters and numbers correctly printed, will aid his memory.

Confusions with **b** and **d** are easily corrected by some children if they are written into the palm of their hands, with the thumbs pointing upwards, the **b** written on the left hand, and the **d** on the right hand.

Figure 9

The **b e d** diagram, which many children find useful, could be made as a rubber stamp and placed at the top of the page in his writing book as a visual aid until the difference between the two letters is learned.

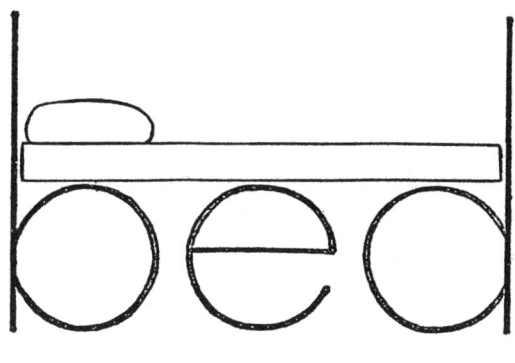

Figure 10

The confusion of the **b** and **d** is less likely to occur in the school system where the Nelson Script is taught because the **b** is written differently and the **d** has a small foot.

b d

Figure 11

It must be remembered that some of these suggestions are perhaps inappropriate in the classroom setting, and may need to be confined to the remedial lessons, or be used at home by parents. When they are used it is essential that they are temporary measures and that the child should not become dependent on them.

Gross motor skills   that are well developed contribute substantially to the child's social adjustment as he is able to participate fully in playground activities and develop confidence arising from peer group recognition, if he is able to do well in sport. This is particularly important to create a balance for the children who are not able to perform well in the class-room.

Visual perceptual and spatial skills   that are well developed, contribute to easier performance in maths.

Memory skills   that are well developed make it easier for children to copy correctly from the blackboard.

Fine motor control   that is well developed facilitates learning to write.

Language and listening skills   that are well developed ensure that the child derives maximum benefit from verbal instructions in the class room.

Children who have lags in the development of any of their perceptual or sensory motor skills are the ones most likely to be educationally at risk.

In conclusion, there is no doubt that children with well developed percerptual and sensory motor skills are better equipped to learn, however, they do still have to be taught.

CHAPTER 6

Strategies for Academic Learning

THE only successful teaching method for the child who is not coping with his school work is to provide instruction at his level of competence, without expecting any chance learning to take place.

The teacher or remediator should take nothing for granted and should have an *"I'll leave nothing to chance"* approach, which can be achieved if the following five principles are adopted, as advocated by Dr Jerome Rosner in his book "Overcoming Learning Difficulties".

FIVE TEACHING PRINCIPLES

❏ Organise for success

This in practical terms means limiting the information being presented at any given time and ensuring that information is presented simply, correctly sequenced, with pertinent points being emphasised by demonstrations and the inclusion of visual clues.

❏ Avoid assumptions

Establish whether he has retained what has been taught previously before introducing new concepts.

❏ Design a strategy

Ensure that what is being taught is making sense to him. Do not leave him to work things out for himself.

Figure 1: *He becomes frustrated if left to work things out for himself*

❏ Encourage the use of all his senses

In addition to visual and auditory stimuli, introduce touch, movement and even smell, when relevant.

Figure 2: *Do not ignore the sense of smell*

❏ Use repetition

Provide sufficient repetitive practice for information to be established securely in the long term memory. He should reach a point where responses are virtually automatic. Short sessions are more effective than long periods of study.

Applying these five principles and referring to them constantly should contribute substantially to a successful outcome when teaching visual learners individually.

SUGGESTIONS TO ENSURE SUCCESS EXPERIENCES

Although learning should be fun, a sense of responsibility must be instilled, where he knows, and is told, that he is being helped to learn to concentrate. He must try to direct his physical abilities and reasoning processes towards a specific goal. It is helpful to state the goal for the child before he begins to work.

The purpose, or aim in teaching is more important than the activity itself. Any game or activity can be selected to achieve the broad principles, which should include teaching time, space, distance, movement and acquisition of language, to ensure that orderly cognitive growth takes place.

All the help given should be preceded by checking that he knows that we live in a "rule governed society". He may need reminders until the rules are internalised and become automatic, for example,

"Before I start this work I need a pencil, a ruler and an eraser".

The remediator or parent states the rules in accordance with the situation until he can apply them independently, bearing in mind that visual learners do not organise themselves well and need, at least initially, to have the structure imposed upon them.

A few useful phrases for him to memorise before he starts his work are:

❏ I must sit up straight and concentrate.

❏ I must think before I ink.

❏ When my work gets better I can tell, it's because I have listened well.

Be sensitive and observant, that is, stop when his interest flags or the task seems too difficult.

Games must be played by the rules because understanding and following the rules are as educational as the game itself.

Time limits, if imposed, should be adjusted to the level of maturity of the players.

It should be remembered that young children are not competitive. For example, if a five year old is playing French cricket with his older siblings, he may, when he has batted and been caught out, refuse to continue the game. As this is age appropriate behaviour, an explanation is better than a reprimand. He should be allowed to withdraw voluntarily but it is important that the game should continue, even if without his presence.

Do not start a game and let it go undirected. Following through to a conclusion is the key to success.

Remember, during play, work, and activities of daily living at home and at school, to apply the three R's, Repetition, Reinforcement and Revue. This should improve his skills and help him to establish good habits and appropriate learning strategies which should in turn result in him performing better.

STRATEGIES FOR SPECIFIC SCHOOL RELATED ACTIVITIES
Handwriting

It is important to make a distinction between written language and writing. The latter is our concern here and refers to the physical act of making marks on paper with a pencil.

Surprising as it may seem, teaching and learning handwriting can and should be enjoyable and easy. The following suggestions should produce a noticeable improvement in a child's handwriting.

At the outset he must be given a thorough knowledge of the principles to be applied. The planning and actions that precede the act of writing are the following:

Bring to the desk a pencil, eraser, sharpener, ruler and paper. It is wise to clear the desk of other objects. Give the visual learner additional clues by asking him whether he has his five objects on the desk and even write a '5' on the blackboard for him. Give him time to check that he has all his requirements.

When he learns to write, the same principles will apply as when he was taught to cut. That is, we begin by showing him how to hold his pencil comfortably, in a tripod grip, with his fingers placed on the shaft of the pencil just where the paint and the wood come together, after the pencil has been well sharpened. The thumb is on the left, the index finger along the top of the shaft and the middle finger rests underneath.

Sometimes the use of a pencil grip is indicated until the correct grip is adopted with ease. It is also important to ensure that he has a correct hand position, with the back of the pencil pointing towards his right shoulder if right handed. If he is left handed, refer to Chapter 9 to ensure that the correct approaches for the left hander are adopted.

Refer to your large illustration which should be prominently displayed and should be a clear diagram of a mature three point pencil grip for both right and left handers.

Figure 3: *Correct paper position for writing with the left hand*

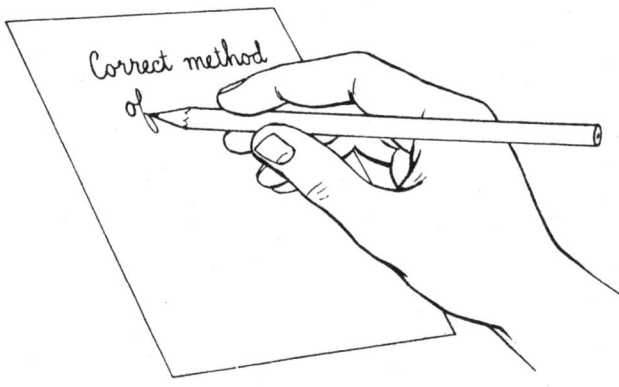

Figure 4: *Correct paper position for writing with the right hand*

Teach him the correct sitting posture, bearing in mind that control of the muscles in writing is dependent on the body weight being correctly distributed. He must sit upright, with the lower back against the back of the seat, with the upper back and shoulders leaning slightly forward.

Figure 5: *Comfortable sitting posture*

Ensure that his elbow is just off the desk, so that the large forearm muscle forms a pivot for the writing movement. Show him how to hold his pencil. *Remember to demonstrate*, as verbal instructions alone discriminate against the visual learner (Appendix, page 150).

Before commencing the lesson review your own guidelines with the child and these should include the following basic principles:

❑ Always insist on precision and accuracy.

❑ Have criteria of acceptability and do not accept anything less.

❑ When not accepting what has been presented, explain why, do not say, "It's untidy", rather say, "the letters touch the baseline, the 'i' must be dotted, the 't' must be crossed. Remember, the limits of acceptability must be challenging, yet achieveable.

❑ Date all samples of work and give him the opportunity to compare his past and present efforts, but excercise caution and make the comparison only when there is visible progress.

❑ Remember that a high degree of structure is called for, with constant and regular practice being the only road to success.

❑ Teach directly: do not rely on incidental learning as children do not "catch" good hand writing. Poor writing habits are not easily broken.

❑ Always use concise relevant instructions and be consistent. Check that you are using the same terminology as his teacher in order to minimise confusion. It is useful to ask his teacher for a sample of the alphabet as she likes to see it written.

❑ Ensure that he understands terms, for example, the word "slant" is appropriate to describe a writing movement but may have to be demonstrated for application.

❑ When describing a writing stroke avoid comments such as, "The fishing line goes right down into the water", it is much better to say, "Slant your line down to the left".

If a child writes slowly, producing mirror images and reversals, it is unwise for the teacher to suggest extra writing practice, or writing lessons, before defining the difficulties. If the child is found to have lags in his understanding of directionality and left-right concepts, then extra lessons will be counter-productive because the symptoms are being addressed without the cause being removed. The consequence of this is that the problem will return or still be there when the lessons are discontinued.

An occupational therapist can assess the child and design an appropriate programme to help develop the skills needed to ensure that, when he is taught to write, he experiences minimal difficulties in the speed and presentation of his work.

As it is very important when teaching writing to ensure that the child has correct starting points when forming letters, an example of the correct formation of all the letters and numbers is given in Appendix, page 155.

A useful strategy to help achieve the right sizing of letters is the use of "kitty lines"

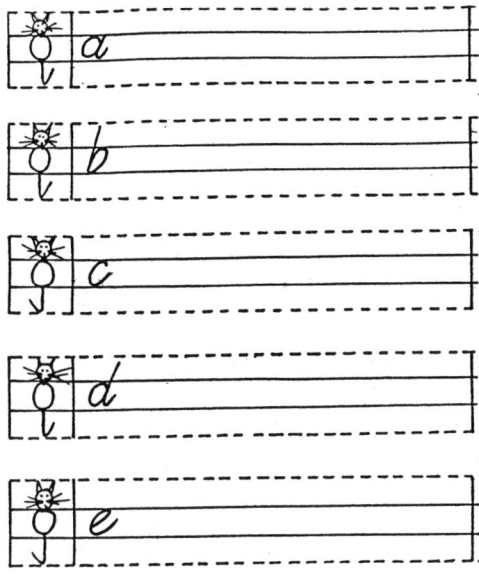

Figure 6: *An example of learning to write the first five letters of the alphabet*

For more detailed guidance in helping children to learn to write, the guide entitled, "The Right Way Up", remediation of hand writing by Claudia Donaldson-Selby, is highly recommended. (Refer to the bibliography).

READING

Every parent and teacher has a unique responsibility to become involved in teaching the child to read, as well as to instil in him the love and appreciation of books and their contents, which will give him the chance to take full advantage of opportunities to acquire knowledge, share opinions and enjoy the pleasure derived from being able to read.

If a child is not learning to read as well as his peers, particularly if his teacher and parents feel that he has good intellectual potential, it is necessary to determine which strategies he is applying when he attempts to read. An assessment which defines his strengths and weaknesses should precede remedial teaching to avoid the situation sometimes encountered, where a child has remedial teaching for a year or more, with limited benefits.

He is then assessed again, only to find that he has poor vision and needs glasses, or has poorly developed pre-reading skills, such as a weak auditory sequential memory, or limited vocabulary, where the help of a language therapist may have been more appropriate.

Starting with a good assessment avoids putting the cart before the horse and ensures that occupational therapy, speech therapy, language enrichment, or psychotherapy precedes the remedial intervention, which will not only increase the likelihood of success in the proposed remedial programme, but could also reduce the time it takes to overcome his reading difficulty.

Parents and teachers will find it easier to help the child to learn to read if they ensure that there are three reading levels constantly in operation. These are

❏ independent level.

❏ instructional level.

❏ frustration level.

The first, the independent level, is where the child reads unassisted for pleasure and makes no errors. For example, if a grade II child wants to read his grade I book, do not say, "That's too easy for you, read the books your teacher has given you", as he needs the repetitive practice which not only improves his reading ability, but also develops his confidence. Some children elect to read the same book over and over and this should not be discouraged.

The second is the instructional level, which is his class level, or his own level of reading, where assistance is needed in the form of supplying the occasional word that he does not know. It is sometimes helpful for the parent or remediator to read one page, then let him read the next page.

It is essential to take into account that when he experiences a reading difficulty, his instructional level may be different from his class level, for example, he may need to be reading grade II level books, although he is already in grade III.

Thirdly, there is the frustration level, where he makes so many errors when reading that it interferes with his comprehension and he becomes agitated. He must be allowed to experience the contents of a book, where the reading may be at his frustration level but the content is at his interest level. This book should be read to him to give him the opportunity of experiencing it, particularly if he has chosen the book himself.

A useful rule of thumb when choosing a book to read, is to ask him to read aloud from any page in the book. If he reads fluently with no errors, the book is at his independent level and he can read it on his own for pleasure.

If he makes three to four errors when reading approximately 15 words, the book is at his instructional level and should be read with him, where he should do most of the reading.

Finally, if he mis-reads five or more words in 15, the book is at his frustration level and must be read to him.

Because parents and teachers do not always apply these levels of reading, children with difficulties are required to read at their frustration level, which may be the instructional level for their peers, who read more fluently.

In addition, many parents with good intentions, say to the child, "It's no good my reading to you because you will never learn to read yourself". The reality is that the child who does not read well needs to be read to, even more than the one who is coping with his reading.

When helping the visual learner, who often does experience difficulties with reading, it is vital to provide opportunities for him to anchor visually and he has to be given visual clues to aid his learning. Do not cover pictures when reading and do not insist on correct word recognition at the expense of comprehension.

For example, if he reads 'a' instead of 'the', ignore the error, as it makes little difference to the meaning of the passage. If he is stopped to re-read, his fluency is interrupted, which in turn interferes with his memory and comprehension.

Another useful hint is to develop a substitute word (let him choose one) to put in the place of words not recognised instantly. Encourage him to use his substitute word and read to the end of the sentence, then go back and possibly say the word from understanding the context, or by using appropriate word attack skills to decipher it. (word attack skills includes the ability to make use of phonic knowledge, breaking into syllables and using other techniques to analyse the words).

For example, for, "the aeroplane makes a loud noise when it flies past", he may read and not recognise the word 'noise'. He should read, "the aeroplane makes a loud *something* when it flies past". The word in italics is the substitute word. He then either recognises the word from comprehending the context, or he can use his phonic knowledge to analyse it.

As many books on reading and teaching of reading, as well as remedial teachers are available to teach reading, only a few indicators are given here to give parents some insight to make them feel confident in their ability to help the child.

Most schools teach reading through a combination of three basic approaches:

❏ the whole word approach
❏ the linguistic approach
❏ the phonic approach.

The whole word (look-say approach) is successful for learning sight words but taxes the memory too heavily to be used in isolation because the most successful system for remembering the spoken, or printed word is by using phonic clues. For example, 'look' can be remembered by it's visual appearance but when confronted by a list of the words, 'took', 'book', 'hook', the likelihood of the learner becoming confused is self evident.

The errors visual learners sometimes make include reading, 'thirty' for 'thirsty', 'carry' for 'canary', and 'begging' for 'beginning'. That is, the visual learner who has not been successful in learning phonics, will resort to using his well developed visual skills and look at the first letter and shape of the word, then guess, and does not apply word attack skills.

The linguistic approach uses rhyming sets such as, cat, rat, hat, bat, fat, which the hard to teach visual learner finds difficult because he lacks the auditory analysis skills to cope with this method. The linguistic approach works well with many children but does not meet the needs of the child who has developmental delays in auditory skills.

The phonic approach , which is regarded by many educators as the method of preference, teaches reading through letter-sound combinations, emphasing the vowel sounds, for example, *ou, oa, ei, ai,* which have single sounds although they each have two letters. Again, this method also has disadvantages because of the irregularities in English, where many words cannot be analysed phonetically.

Reading is taught in a sequential manner, that is, opposite to the ideal rapid recognition of words as a whole. All children need to be exposed to some phonic teaching and with the visual learner, it is helpful to introduce the concept of *seeing* the sounds.

For example, when learning the word *boat,* present it visually on the blackboard as, *b-oa-t.* Then say to him, "The word *boat* has three sounds", point to each, saying it's sound. Tell him that there are four letters but only three sounds.

It is essential for him to appreciate the concept of sound combinations, as it is impossible to blend if he sounds out the letters individually, that is, saying, *h-o-u-s-e* makes it difficult, if not impossible, to blend these sounds to make the word. It has been observed that many parents are confused because they think their children know their phonics when they can recognise the sound for each letter of the alphabet. They are not taking into account that there are only *five vowels*, but seventeen *vowel-sound* combinations, which takes the number of sounds up to at least forty six or more, depending on the specific phonic method that has been selected.

There is no single method that will work perfectly for every child.

MODALITY PREFERENCE

Modality preference refers to the fact that reading is the conversion of symbols into language when a whole word approach to reading is advocated for a poor reader, because he has been identified as a visual learner. It must be emphasised that *one* approach, which excludes other methods, is not likely to be successful.

A multi-sensory approach can be helpful and creative innovations such as colour coding should be used but only as a temporary measure, to be discarded as soon as the transition has been made to enable him to cope without the additional support.

In conclusion, there is only one way to teach reading. Have a frame of reference which provides on target instruction, which ensures that the child can convert symbols into language. Apply the five principles of good teaching described at the beginning of this chapter.

It is up to the teacher and the parent or remedial teacher to adopt methods that suit each child's learning style.

PHONICS, SPELLING AND WRITTEN LANGUAGE

These three are presented in the sequence given. Phonics is more important for spelling, than for reading. A child who has a sound phonic knowledge finds it easier to spell well, and the child with good spelling ability is usually able to express himself in the written form with ease, accuracy and fluency.

PHONICS

Many visual learners have difficulty acquiring good phonic knowledge because the skills required to cope with learning phonics are auditory and include discrimination, sequencing, memory and closure.

The essence of phonics is to break words up into their sounds whilst the visual learner prefers to learn by a whole word approach. As the visual recognition of the whole word is his preferred learning style, he avoids applying his phonic knowledge.

It is helpful when teaching phonics to the visual learner, to colour code the vowel sounds to emphasise them, and it is also helpful for some children if the sounds are numbered and separated. For example, if the word *throat* is being learned, *thr* are numbered *1*, the *oa* are colour coded and separated as number *2* and the *t* is numbered *3* and written separately.

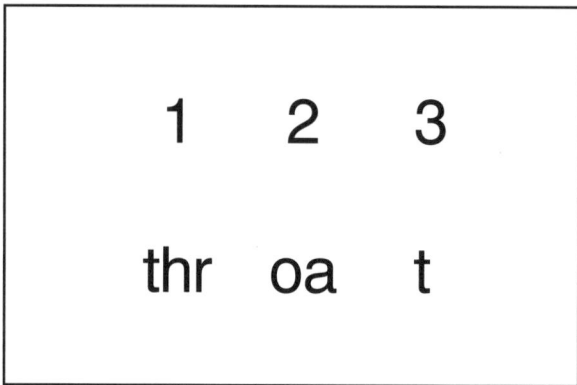

Figure 7

It is then explained to him while he is looking at it, that although the word has six letters, there are only three sounds.

As it is outside the purpose of this book to teach phonics, the authors suggest use of a phonics hand-book called, "Breaking the Sound Barrier" by Sister Mary Caroline. (See bibliography).

SPELLING

With the rapid changes taking place in our educational system and with the advent of computers and their spelling checks, there is no longer the same emphasis on correct spelling, as in the past.

Teachers should however endeavour to maintain acceptable standards. They need to be flexible when judging the written work of the visual learners, who are often unable to spell well, and even as adults may still have difficulty with spelling.

Spelling errors should NEVER be overlooked. However, a lower mark for a piece of creative writing should not always be given because of spelling errors. Bizarre errors which interfere with the meaning or context of the work cannot be accepted but there are many acceptable alternatives, such as writing *color* for *colour*.

As proficiency in reading, ability to write well and mastery of phonics are needed before the learner is able to spell efficiently, he may not cope with spelling before reaching Grade III.

Because most children learn to spell well with ease, parents and teachers are often frustrated by the visual learner, who, despite all attempts to teach him, fails to spell well.

However, if it is taken into account that to spell, he must be able to automatically and spontaneously write any letter of the alphabet which entails remembering what it looks like (visualisation), remembering what it sounds like (auditorisation), and making the marks on the page which accurately represent it's appearance (write it). The appreciation of the complexity of the process will make it easier for us as teachers and parents, to help him and also to be more tolerant of his shortcomings.

Our purpose here is not to teach spelling but to offer some suggestions to add to those that are presently being used by teachers and parents.

Consider the following, firstly, as it is not uncommon for a child to spell a word correctly out aloud, then write it down incorrectly, it is essential to establish the following rule firmly,

"You have to write out every word in full when you learn it, and sometimes new words will have to be written many times".

Accept that the only successful methods are tedious, boring, repetitive and time consuming which means setting aside sufficient time to complete the whole process of learning the word and providing appropriate incentives to maintain motivation.

A poor speller usually needs to use a multisensory approach where he is able to see and hear, as well as say and write the word.

There are many teachers who provide each child with a

s a c a w a c

<u>s</u>tudy the word
<u>and</u>
<u>c</u>over the word
<u>and</u>
<u>w</u>rite the word
<u>and</u>
<u>c</u>heck the word

Figure 8

HINTS FOR BETTER SPELLING

Make sure that the child knows his alphabet and can use it, particularly for looking up his words in a dictionary.

Encourage him to break the word into parts, for example, wonderful = *won der ful.*

Suggest that he uses his brain like a camera to photograph new words by closing his eyes and trying to see the new word in his mind.

Encourage him to pay attention to words which obey spelling rules and then to learn the exceptions, for example,

The i sound at the end of a word is usually y, except in

coffee,
taxi,
spaghetti,
committee.

Teach only the simpler spelling rules with care and be consistent, for example, one Grade VI pupil was taught the rule,

When making the plural for a word that ends in 'y', drop the 'y' and add, 'ies'.

When asked to spell the word *'babies'* the following week, he wrote,

bab ies

y

saying, I remembered the rule, you told me to 'drop' the 'y' and add 'ies'. Encourage him to play games, do crosswords, enter spelling competitions and when given a long word, such as, rhinoceros, ask him how many words he can make, using the letters in the word.

Examples of useful games are, Scrabble, Spin and Spell, Boggle, and Bingo.

Encourage him to make up nonsense rhymes or phrases to remember the non-phonetic, irregular or tricky words, for example,

'possesses, possesses, five esses'

'Sue-Anne uses 'sage' to make 'sausage''

Remember that it is not sufficient to know how to spell a word, he must be able to pronounce it correctly, know what it means and use it in a sentence.

It is unfortunate, but drill sessions have to be continued with all words, until they can be spelled automatically. The child can be encouraged by introducing incentives.

INCENTIVES

When marking the spelling of words, give a point for each letter that is in the correct place, for example,

'friend' written as 'freind'

will give him four points. All his points are added together with a goal for the maximum number of points, which can be used at the end of the week for a special privilege, for example, to stay up late for a TV show, or go on a visit of his choice, such as going to the beach, the animal farm or snake park.

Graphs are also useful as he then has a visual record of his progress.

Older children can also be given an index box with two sets of cards, where the words being learned are placed alphabetically on the front card, and once they have been learned and written correctly, three times consecutively, they are placed at the back of the pack, known as the 'bank', which earns him a ten cent piece which he 'banks' in a small plastic container, for example, a capsule phial.

At a later stage he is told that he can cash up, which means that he is given a test of the words in the bank and if he then makes any errors, he has to 'pay back' at a coin for each mistake. If, however, he makes no errors, he keeps the money. The whole process can then be repeated for another set of words.

When all else has failed, try the following procedure:

Write the word that is to be learned on a large piece of paper. Let the child say the word, pronouncing each letter. Ask him to copy the word, saying each letter out aloud and repeat this step five times.

Ask him to write the word from memory, still saying each letter out aloud and repeat the process five times.

Ask him to close his eyes and with his eyes closed, write the word five times, spelling it out aloud as he writes it.

Then ask him to write the word, using it in its correct context and explain that it is more beneficial if he is able to make up his own sentence.

Provided there is a positive approach and attitude on the part of the parents and teachers, the majority of children should learn to spell well enough to ensure that the presentation of their written work is acceptable.

EXPRESSING ONESELF IN WRITTEN LANGUAGE

It is not uncommon for parents to become upset when they are told for the first time, when their child is perhaps already in Grade III, that he has a written language disability. This is usually not due to negligence on the part of the teacher or the school, but due to the nature of the problem, as written language is the last stage in the acquisition of learning skills related to language. That is, he first learns to read, then to write, then to spell and apply phonics and finally, all these processes culminate in his ability to produce a passage of written work.

A discussion of specific written language disabilities is outside the scope of this guide but some visual learners and certain children with specific language disabilities, have difficulty coping with their written work. It is important to identify the differences in the types of written samples produced by the two groups of children.

The child with a specific language disability is unable to express his thoughts on paper in a legible or understandable way, but can himself, read and correctly relate what he has written. The visual learner on the other hand, usually writes a story that is shorter, with poor spelling and untidy writing, but it is legible and comprehensible, that is, it can be read and understood without reference to the writer.

The example below illustrates the two responses to the request to "write about your visit to the air show in Johannesburg". The boy with the language disability has no difficulty reading his story as follows, "I went to Johburg, my aunt and me went to the air show and we saw the Red Arrows". The visual learner was, on the other hand, more hesitant with the reading of his story, although it was a more acceptable and more legible sample of writing.

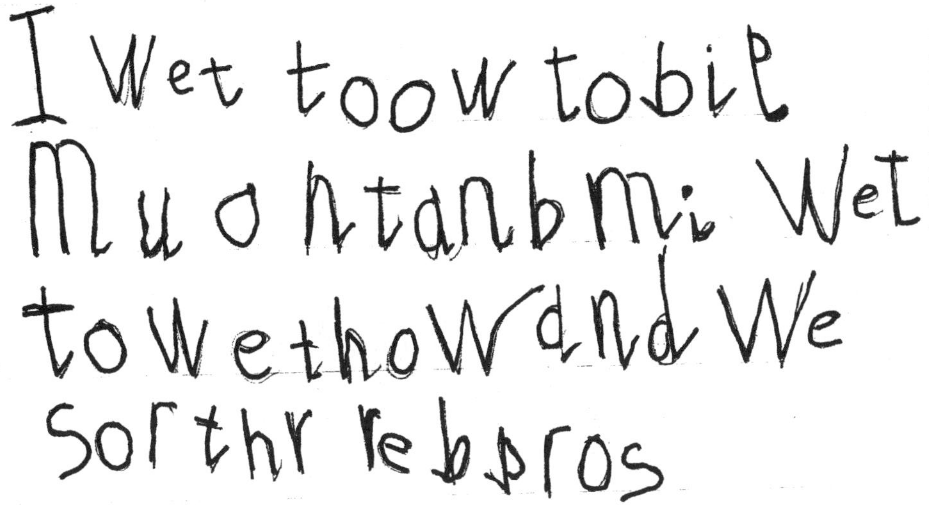

I Wet toow tobil
Muontanbmi Wet
toWethoWand We
Sorthr lebbros

Figure 9: *He has a written language disability*

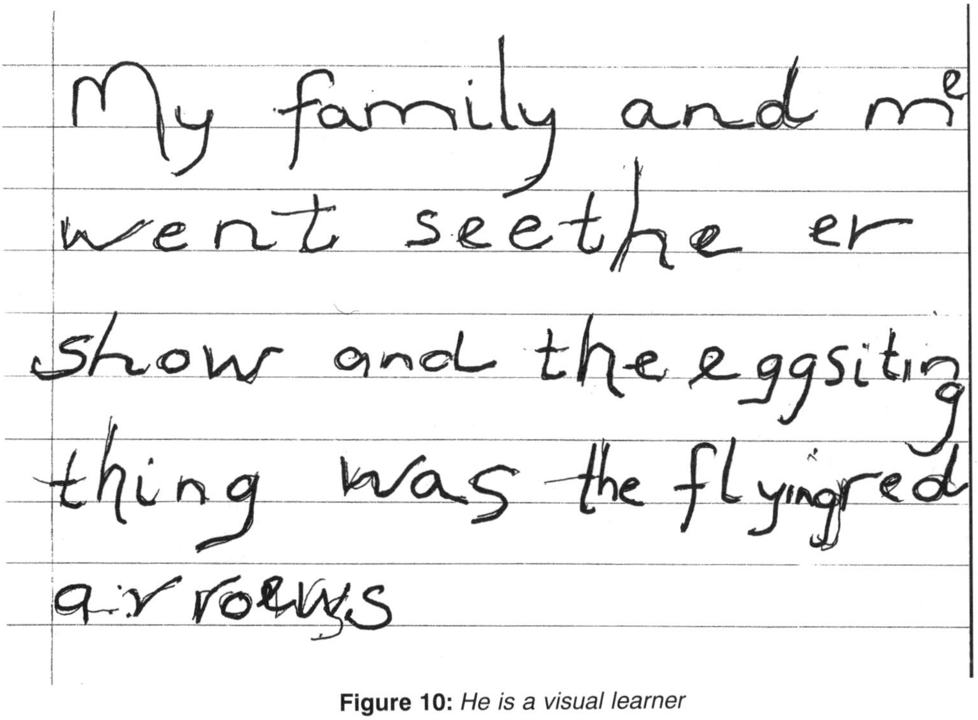

My family and me
went seethe er
show and the eggsiting
thing was the flyingred
arroews

Figure 10: *He is a visual learner*

Many visual learners, when asked to write, will say "I don't know what to write". One boy was encouraged to write his story about a helicopter by first suggesting to him that because he draws well, he should try to draw a helicopter using words as the outline of his picture.

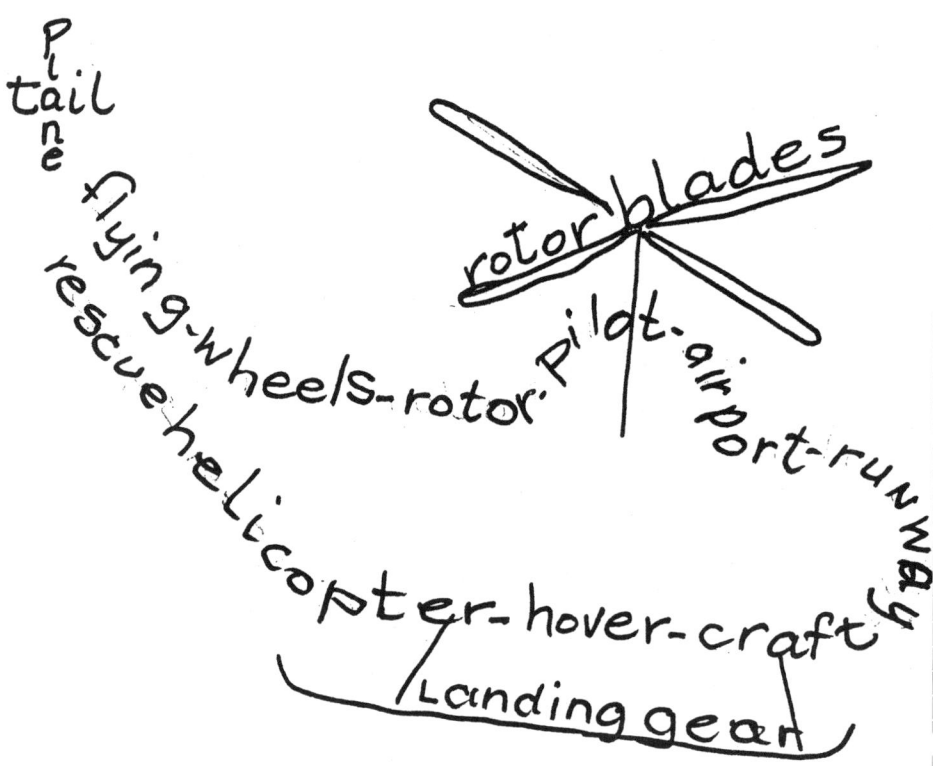

Figure 11: *Helicopter*

The next stage was to encourage him to arrange those words sequentially into a story, indicating to him that he may need to add more words to 'fill out' his story. In this way he wrote a creative story because he was motivated by the drawing.

An experienced language teacher uses the following steps:

❏ Stimulation phase, where there is an oral interchange by

listening and asking questions. For example, "What did you see The Red Arrows doing?".

❏ Providing key words. The teacher assists the learner by enlisting words appropriately. For example, Concorde, military plane, Red Arrows.

❏ The learner writes one or two sentences using the key words.

❏ Final stage involves showing the learner how to connect sentences to produce the story.

COMPREHENSION

There are some visual learners who are labelled as having poor comprehension, when the reality is that they are having difficulty with verbal processing. If the information required could be accessed differently, in a manner which is in keeping with their learning style, they would have a better opportunity of understanding. When questions are to be answered in a comprehension test, a useful technique is to encourage the child to read the question before he reads the story, he then focuses his attention more accurately as he realises the question has a purpose. As many visual learners have difficulty in adopting an orderly approach to their work, it is often beneficial to provide excercises in sequencing events correctly, before expecting good performance in comprehension tests. Visual learners also perform better on comprehension tests where the stories are illustrated, as they are able to take advantage of the additional clues provided by the pictures. Teachers should put extra effort into ensuring that they present information in a manner which makes it easier for all the children to understand and interpret instructions correctly. Teachers and parents should also remind themselves that difficulties experienced in comprehension place severe limits on the child's ability to learn.

Sue Hanauer, in a letter to *The New York Times*, said:

"Improving our children's writing skills must begin at home. We must speak with and read to our children, plan our days to allow time for conversation, teach our children the value of writing a letter rather than using the telephone and limit our children's television time. We will then see an improvement in reading and writing skills, and we will encourage a resurgence of our young people's creative abilities as well".

MATHS

There is new hope for all visual learners, thanks to the new approach to mathematics which has been introduced in many South African schools.

In this system children are encouraged to use their innate creative talents to solve mathematical problems in a variety of ways. There are no restrictions on their use of concrete aids, or movement.

The success of the new approach is dependent on a positive attitude on the part of parents, teachers and mediators. Provided the mediators have a strong conviction that every child possesses basic logical reasoning and the ability to manipulate number concepts far beyond what was previously believed to be possible, many doors will open for children in our schools, particularly the visual learners, who, have often not been able to realise their potential because the system was not accommodating their learning style.

THE MATHEMATICAL MYTH

A poor maths test result does not always reflect a lack of mathematical ability. There are too many children who say, "I cannot do maths", "I'm no good at maths, I never have been and never will be", "I'm just not a maths person".

With maths, more than any other subject, it is essential to instil confidence in him, which is achieved more easily if you, as the teacher or parent, can fully convince him that you have faith in his ability to do maths.

$a^2 + b^4 = 1 \, dog$

Figure 12: *Maths blows my mind*

Basic number facts

Irrespective of the approach or teaching methods used, there is a basic set of number facts which have to be memorised and learned to a point where the child will be able to supply the answer to any problem presented, automatically and spontaneously, without thinking or working it out. This comes with extended practice and drill sessions, there are no short cuts.

When Gary Player was approached with the comment, "I envy you because you are lucky to be such a good golfer", his reply was, "What I've discovered is that the harder I practice, the luckier I become".

As with reading, where the process started with checking that the child is familiar with every single letter of the alphabet, maths help also starts with checking that he is thoroughly familiar with all the numbers, from 0 to 9. The steps are:

❑ matching numbers
❑ pointing to any number on request

❏ naming numbers correctly when presented in random order
❏ printing numbers from dictation and out of sequence.

If young children can be helped to master the concept that maths calculations are multidirectional, they have crossed a huge barrier on the road to success. They need to understand that number sequences can be changed without altering the essence of the problem, that is, '5 plus 4' is the same as '4 plus 5' is the same as '3 plus 2 plus 4' is the same as '4 minus 2 plus 7'.

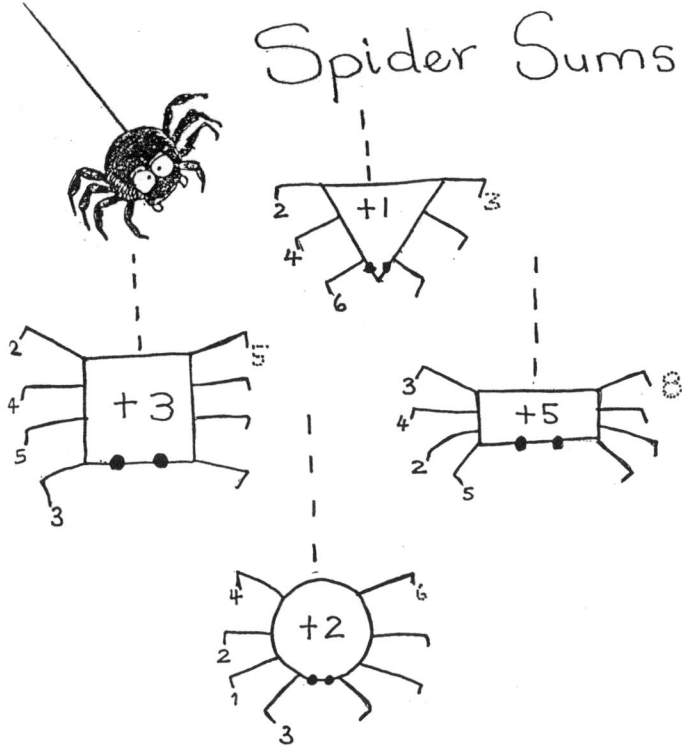

Figure 13: *Spider sums*

Story sums

If teachers recognise that visual learners have marked difficulty coping with number and word concepts simultaneously, they will find it easier to help these children find solutions when doing story sums.

When helping the child who has difficulty doing story sums, encourage him to verbalise what he is doing, in order to help you observe his method of working. The sum can then be broken down into manageable chunks. In addition, he can be helped to find key-words that determine which operation (addition, subtraction, multiplication or division) he needs to use.

It is vital to ensure that instructions are explicit and concise. A teacher once told the author about a little boy who had complained about having difficulty with multiplication, to which she replied, "But multiplication is so easy, it's just a series of additions". His response was a hearty laugh followed by, "I think I've heard that joke somewhere before".

Story sum example

The teacher begins with, "I will show you a way to remember how to multiply". Your sum says, "John has three bags of marbles with seven marbles in each bag, how many marbles does he have altogether?". You may find it easier to draw the sum, then say to him, "Now you can count them and you can also see for yourself that multiplication is a quick way of adding".

John had three bags of marbles. Each bag had seven in it. How many marbles did John have?

$$3 \times 7 = 21$$

Figure 14

In conclusion, it is our plea to educational authorities, specifically regarding students' inability to produce acceptable written assignments, to provide opportunities for greater time allotments, oral examinations, and spelling exemption certificates to be given to examiners, and, separate writing space, so as not to disturb others when there is a need to auditorise (talk to one's self when writing).

Above all, we request flexibility in the system to enable the teachers to avoid making demands on the children that are beyond their integrative capacities.

CHAPTER 7

Strategies and Study Techniques for the Visual Learner

IF THE teacher is able to recognise the visual learner in her classroom and knows his traits, this prepares her to make constructive suggestions when his parents approach her with,

"What should I, as a parent, be doing to help my child?".

An appropriate response would be:

He is a visual learner and as they are known to be physically active and creative by nature, you could perhaps encourage him to join the computer or chess club, or enrol him in art classes or music lessons. Let him swim or play tennis, or practice karate. If he can excel in any of these or similar activities, it will be a wonderful confidence booster for him".

One of the authors worked with a dyslexic boy who was a talented cricketer and she recalls his parents arriving with his school report to substantiate their claim that:

"Apart from the fact that he always gains significantly in his level of confidence, all his marks on his school report improve considerably as soon as the cricket season starts".

Teachers should not underestimate the enormous power they have over the children in their classrooms. Parents often say to us,

"His teacher's word is law in our house, she is never wrong".

Haven't you, as teachers, heard the following plea from a parent,

"I really would like you to tell him because he never listens to us"

It is appropriate to quote the view of Mary Hudson, the author of Nicola books, who said;

"Children with learning difficulties become overwhelmed by their lack of achievement and they lose confidence in themselves. Visual learners are imaginative and creative and through the medium of mime, dance, speech and drama, all right brain states, they become more confident and motivated to try harder to achieve and improve their communication skills"

Through the years we have often recommended that children be enrolled for speech and drama classes. There is wide support amongst parents and where children have indeed benefitted from such training, there are observable improvements in their communication skills. We endorse the views of Mary Hudson and Professr Sneddon, amongst others, who believe that speech and drama should be included in the school curriculum.

On the other hand, nothing prevents teachers from introducing in their language and other lessons, the acting out of scenes if they feel comfortable in so doing.

HOW A TEACHER CAN IMPROVE HER OWN SKILLS

For the teacher who is motivated and interested in helping visual learners, there are many courses and books available on the subject. Two suggestions are; attending Theme Programming Workshops or enrolling for Education in Human Values training. The former are workshops for teachers which aim to integrate physical education, language, drama, dance and music into general education curricula.

The latter is an approach which is used world wide to build confidence, self esteem and morale. The techniques embody intellectual, physical, psychical, emotional and spiritual aspects of human development. Teachers are trained to incorporate all these values into their classroom teaching (Appendix, page 146).

Our present school system places emphasis on physical and intellectual growth, with the growth of emotional, psychical and spiritual needs sometimes being neglected. (for further details refer to the last paragraph in this chapter).

CLASSROOM SUGGESTIONS

❏ The teacher who provides visual stimuli and opportunities for movement has already made a major contribution towards helping the visual learner in her classroom.

❏ For the older child the teacher is well advised to call him aside to discuss his difficulties. It is not enough for a parent to say, "Don't worry, your teacher knows you've got a problem". He needs to hear it from his teacher.

❏ It is sometimes necessary to place the child near the teacher's desk but the arrangement should include an incentive for him to work towards returning to his original place. Focussing too much attention on him over a long period of time could be counter-productive.

❑ Reduce pressure of time and competition in the classroom, speed need not be emphasised at the expense of neatness. Many children regard being first to finish as more important than presenting tidy, correct work.

❑ Be on the look-out for avoidance tactics, such as deliberately producing illegible writing, so that errors are not detected.

❑ The use of red pens when marking books is not in keeping with the goal, which is to be realistic but not demoralising, when identifying errors.

❑ A comment regarding the content of his work is preferable to numerous crosses, for example, rather than six red crosses, say, "I can see that you have tried hard and now I will help you to correct the errors".

❑ Aids, such as an alphabet card, a small number chart, a pencil grip or book-marks, should be permitted because they help the child to focus on the task, rather than on the mechanics of working. They should, however, be used temporarily, with praise being given when he is able to discard them.

❑ Enlist the help of parents, for example, give them suggestions that are specific, such as, "Read his homework to him", rather than to say, "It's your work, and it's no use if I have to read it to you because you will never learn to read yourself".

❑ Setting up a quiet corner in the back of the classroom, with a bookshelf as a barrier, with only a desk and chair, could be effective. The children go there on their own to complete work if they are being distracted. It is not used for punishment but the wise teacher should be able to encourage the visual learners and attention deficit children to make use of it.

❑ Some Grade I left-handers are desperately in need of space and may have a more positive start to their schooling if they are, at least in the beginning, permitted to have their own desks.

❑ When appropriate, lessons conducted outdoors can be beneficial for all the children.

❑ Teachers need to know that the majority of children do not respond to loud voices. Shouting is not an effective disciplinary tool. When one of the authors visited schools and homes in the United States, she accompanied a speech therapist who had a portable audiometer and was measuring decibel levels. The levels that she recorded of teachers voices in the classroom and parents shouting in their homes, were in some instances beyond the pain threshold. She also mentioned an incident where a teacher had actually burst a child's ear drum by shouting suddenly right next to him.

STUDY SKILLS FOR VISUAL LEARNERS

The techniques described in this section are suitable for children with poor listening skills, namely, right brain dominant, epileptic, gifted and hard of hearing scholars. In a language orientated classroom they are expected to listen, express themselves in oral or written language and to study from written notes. One can equate this to that of a right footed soccer player being told to use his left foot on the field. It can be done, but it is not easy and does not utilise his ability. It is therefore necessary to equip the visual learner with techniques to learn, where he can make use of his inherent well developed visual skills.

❑ The visual learner is a poor listener and processes language slowly. He retains information best from diagrams, pictures, maps, dramatic presentations, acting out, music and rhythm. When he receives remediation for his weak areas, he should at the same time be encouraged to compensate with his well developed right brain skills. He should be allowed to use his good visual skills confidently with no attempt being made to change him into an auditory learner.

❑ In the first instance one should be sure that hearing and vision are intact. An audiologist should assess hearing and a paediatric optometrist should test vision.

❑ Being a visual learner does not exclude visual problems and the paediatric optometrist looks at those functions which are necessary for learning. Children with learning difficulties frequently have poor accomodative-convergence reflexes and experience difficulty with reading and similar tasks. Accomodation acts to preserve the clarity of an image and convergence to preserve the fusion of the two images into one percept. Optometric vision therapy is a straight forward procedure to re-establish the reflex and if visual training is prescribed the course should be followed through, as concentration improves when the visual stress is reduced. For remediation there are the following facilities:

- Speech therapy for developing language, vocabulary, comprehension, verbal and written expression, auditory discrimination, sequencing and listening skills.
- Occupational therapy for developing visual perception, memory and gross and fine motor co-ordination, as well as encouraging the development of good bilateral integration and the understanding of directional and left-right concepts, particulary as they relate to the correct orientation of letters and numbers.
- Remedial tuition using visual strategies to improve reading, spelling, written expression and maths.

TECHNIQUES THAT TEACHERS AND PARENTS CAN USE

❑ First and foremost, always make eye contact with the child and follow the **KISS** principle,

KEEP IT SHORT AND SIMPLE

To facilitate this in a group situation, particularly in Grade I, it is suggested that the pupils be seated in a V or U formation, so that each child faces the teacher. The use of hexagonal desks is also an effective seating arrangement which facilitates eye contact with the teacher.

❑ Make use of flash cards for reading, spelling and phonics and use visual material to match the sounds. Often visual techniques are used for reading but spelling is taught phonetically. A multi-sensory approach, such as Funkey card games, can be used effectively with visual learners (Appendix, page 147).

❑ Encourage reading books with pictures and with subject matter that can be visualised. Reluctant readers prefer factual books, encyclopaedias and adventure stories.

❑ Use theatrical presentations, films and videos of set books and subject matter, for example, historical stories.

❑ Act out subject matter in a group, or individually, movement and gestures are fun and leave a lasting impression.

❑ Use rhythm for rote learning, for example, tables to music. Some visual learners enjoy poetry because of the rhythm (Appendix, page 146).

❑ Arrange outings to relevant places of interest.

- ❏ Using a word processor enables the child to see what he has written and to correct his spelling.

- ❏ Allow the child to present his work by means of drawings, maps, tables or labelled diagrams. Example; one boy cut out a picture of a plough from a magazine to help him remember the abstract term: "arable land".

- ❏ Tabulated information is easier to learn than that written out in text, provided the lesson has covered the information.

- ❏ Mnenomics are useful, for example, the mnenomic for remembering how to spell 'because' is, 'Betty eats cake and Uncle sells eggs'.

Visual material can be used effectively to teach a language as illustrated in Bev Muller's book, "Sanibona".

Figure 1: *Izithelo*

- ❏ Mindmaps, trigger charts and spider diagrams are a useful way to prepare for exams. (see Chapter 8) and "Brain Power for Kids".

Brain Power for Kids

On this page is a Mind Map of half a year of advanced high school chemistry. Not only is this an example of how to Mind map notes, but also how to face exams. This Mind map was reviewed every two to three weeks for five minutes by a high school student. By the time mid-terms came around, the student hardly had to study and was rewarded with an A.

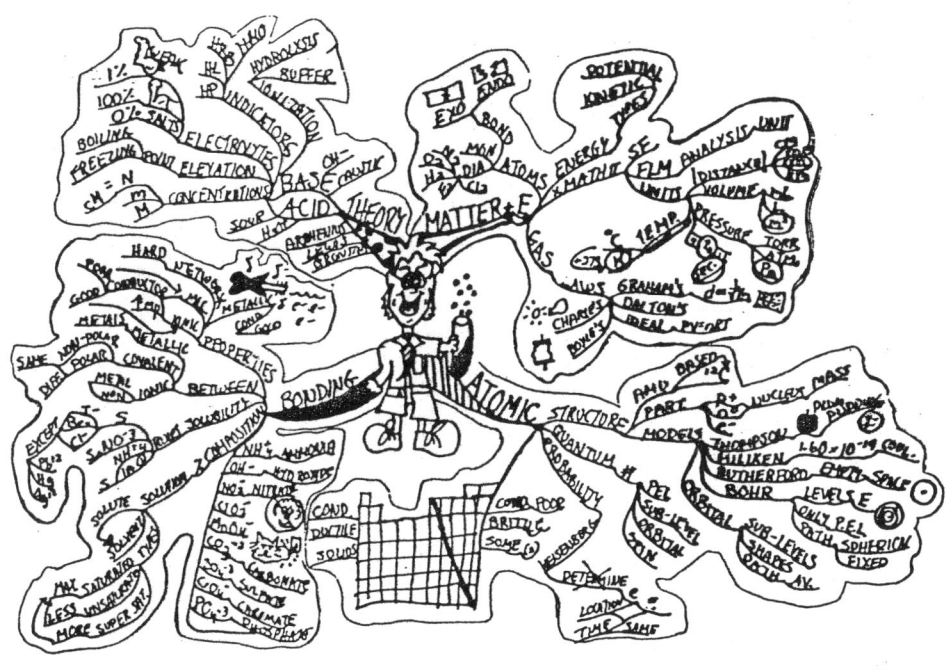

Figure 2: *Mind Map of a half a year of advanced high school chemistry*

☐ Art therapy benefits the visual learner and he enjoys it, which boosts his self image. Betty Edwards said that learning to draw improves right brain skills and that there is a carry over to the left hemisphere which can improve reading and maths. Paulette Dubayle-Barker, a well known artist, used Betty Edwards' drawing methods for a group of visual learners aged between seven and twelve years who were referred to her by the authors. Initially she found the children to be restless, slow, attention seeking and inattentive but as the classes progressed they became confident and motivated, which also carried over into the home and school. They began to express themselves in their newfound creativity and developed a sense of worth. Some of them showed talents which had not previously been recognised. It was sad to note that when she asked them to tell her what they regarded as the most important thing in their lives, the unanimous answer was, "To please our parents and teachers", which meant to do well in class and preferably be near the top. Unfortunately, none of them felt able to achieve this goal.

☐ Although visual techniques for studying draw on the right hemisphere, the left is also involved because the brain works as a whole.

99

Creative Study Methods are particularly effective for visual learners (Appendix, page 146).

❏ An example of visual presentation of material to be learned is the use of an overhead projector in a history lesson. A high school teacher used this technique with an extra-mural group of Grade nine pupils.

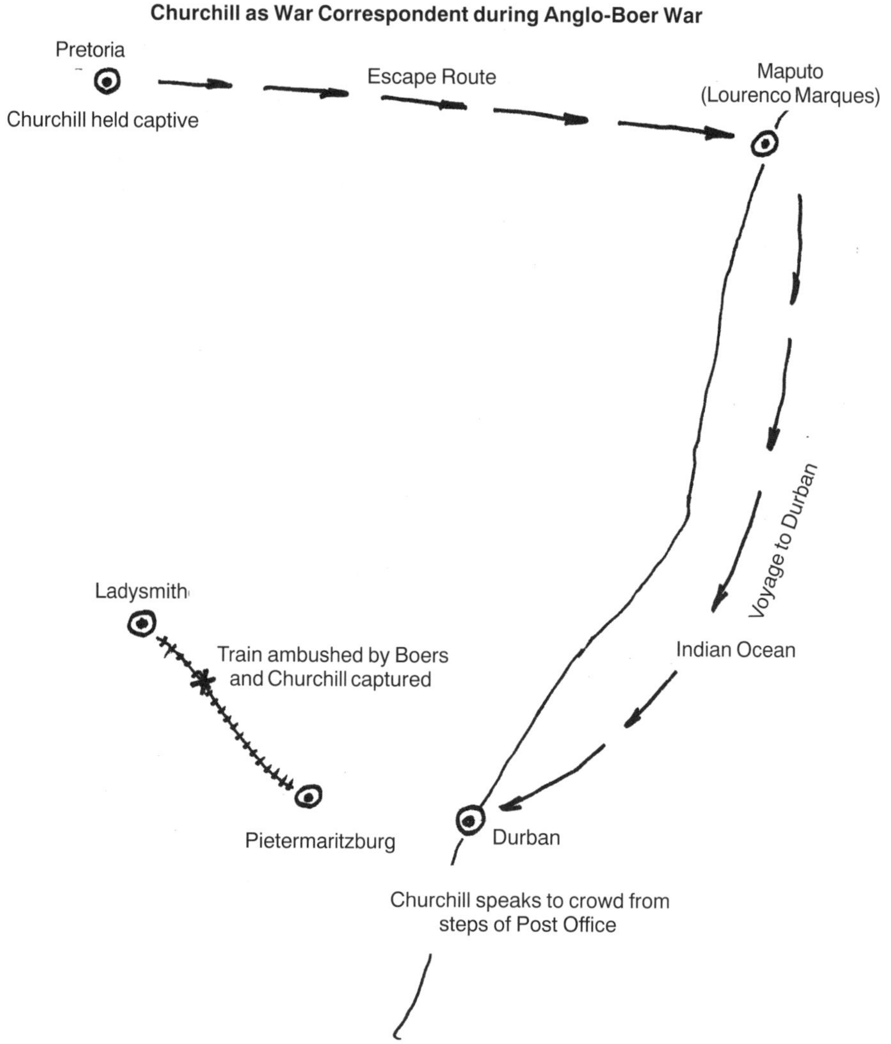

Churchill as War Correspondent during Anglo-Boer War

Pretoria

Churchill held captive

Escape Route

Maputo
(Lourenco Marques)

Ladysmith

Train ambushed by Boers
and Churchill captured

Indian Ocean

Voyage to Durban

Pietermaritzburg

Durban

Churchill speaks to crowd from
steps of Post Office

Figure 3: *Churchill's escape during Anglo-Boer war*

She compared her results on a written test, after each lesson, with tests done in the classroom based on learning from notes. The marks in her group were higher, motivation and concentration were better and there was a carry over of confidence as well as a more positive attitude in the classroom. In her class, where the children were thinking in the right hemisphere mode as they concentrated on visual material, one lad started to draw a map instead of writing a passage in the test. He was allowed to continue which enabled him to produce more information than he would have done in a written passage. They also found it easier to learn from information presented in colour.

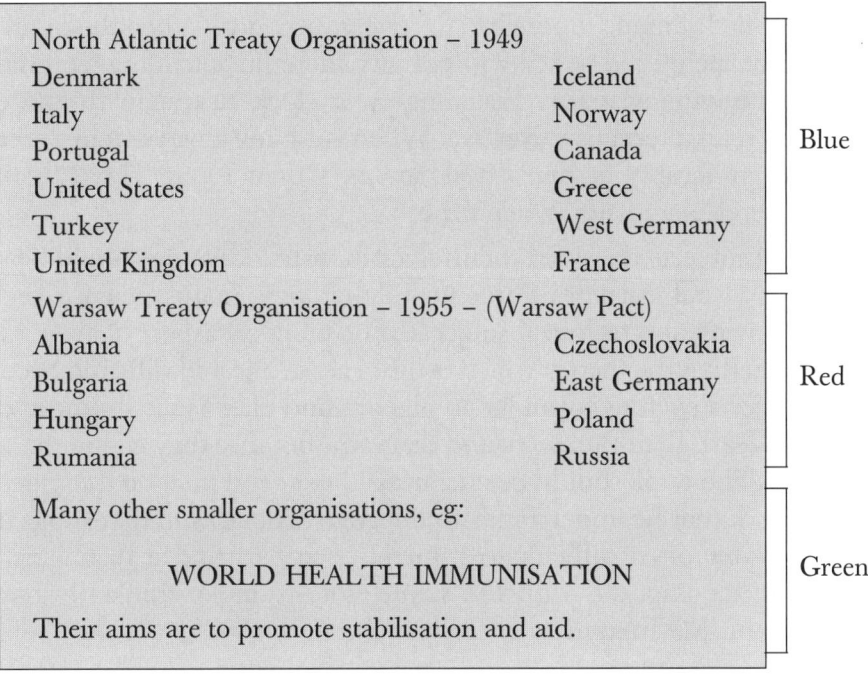

Figure 4: *Tabulated information preferably presented in colour facilitates learning*

❑ When verbal material has to be read, learned or written, the left hemisphere can concentrate only if the more efficient right side does not interfere, which can be achieved by playing Baroque music in the background. The right side will listen, leaving the left side free to pay attention to the language. The rhythm should be sixty beats a minute. The choice of music has nothing to do with personal taste and is not so much background music as it is like a mantra, used to produce a state of relaxed concentration. Music with a slow, constant, monotonous rhythm is not distracting and has the best results. Vocal music is not suitable because the words compete with the text being learned. Bach and Vivaldi have composed suitable largo music. (For details refer to bibliography, Ostrander and Schroeder "Superlearning").

❑ Although visual learners understand mindmapping techniques and enjoy them, they find them difficult to apply. It is not easy to switch to right brain thinking in a left brain environment and practice is necessary for it to become automatic, much like learning to drive a car. A useful exercise to make the transition from left to right brain thinking is to sit in a comfortable chair, back straight, feet flat on the floor, palms resting on the thighs, eyes closed and concentrate on breathing; when relaxed fix the gaze on a pencil held at arms length and look at it, without blinking if possible, for twelve seconds. When the mind can concentrate on the pencil without any thoughts intruding, commence with studying visually. Listening to a clock ticking with the eyes closed is an alternative exercise. When studying always sit in the same place, preferably at one's desk in one's own room. Have frequent short breaks and stop when tired.

❑ School subjects that lend themselves to visual learning should be chosen by visual learners. These include biology, maths, science, technical drawing and technical subjects. The practical aspect of art is easier to learn than the theory which is more academic and difficult. Sections of subjects such as formulae in algebra and chemistry are more difficult to learn than geometry and diagrams because they cannot be visualised. The pupil should be encouraged to spend time on the aspect of the work that he understands to improve his marks in that subject. As names are often difficult to remember, try to find a distinguishing feature to associate with the name, for example, think of shaving cream for Mr Ingram.

❑ Encourage hobbies, interests, sports and physical exercise and do not insist that extra school work at home replaces sport. A child who is struggling with his school work will not achieve any more by sitting for a long period as he will get tired and his concentration will waver. Remember, *It is not the hours that you 'put in' . . . it is what you 'put in' the hours!*

❑ Do not tell a child he is right brain dominant as he may think that there is something wrong with his brain. Call him a visual learner and explain to him that he has a different but not inferior way of learning. He should also be reminded that there are many others like him and that, in important ways, it is a gift.

❑ Ultimately the child should take responsibility for his own learning and develop his own coping skills. He should be discouraged from blaming the system or expecting his parents to do his studying for him.

Figure 5: *"When you have finished your cell-phone conversation, do you think you could help me with your homework?"*

A NEW APPROACH TO EDUCATION IN THE U.S.A.

In an article entitled "Teaching That Goes Beyond I.Q." by Elaine Woo, she describes how doors are opening for some children in the United States of America, because of a new approach in education, based on Gardner's Theory of Multiple Intelligences.

She says "Children stumped by traditional education may flourish with lessons geared to musical and spatial skills. Gardner, who is advancing the theory of Multiple Intelligences, recognises the importance of mathematical and linguistic competence, as the two skill areas most valued in, and measured by our schools, but says, there are also other competencies that are very important in human life as well".

She hopes that this theory will personalise education, which she says is at present based on the assumption that all children must learn the same way.

Seven kinds of intelligence would allow seven ways to teach, rather than one, said Gardner in his book, "Frames of Mind", which describes his theory. Although there is still not sufficient evidence of its effectiveness for the theory to be applied widely, a significant observation is its impact on school attendance rate, which, at 97 percent, is four points higher that the state average, where the survey was done, with a comment from one of the teachers being, "Something is happening at these schools that causes the kids to want to come".

EDUCATION IN HUMAN VALUES

Much has been said about the child, the scholar, but we must not forget the child, the person. EHV (Education in Human Values) is a programme used in schools in many countries which takes into account the intellectual, physical, and spiritual needs of the child by introducing the concepts of, "truth", "righteous conduct", "love", "peace", and "non violence". These five values are integrated into the educational system and can be incorporated into classroom lessons. By addressing the whole child this system enhances memory and fulfils emotional needs and is therapeutic in healing children who are the victims of violence. All religions and cultures are represented. The programme encourages the use of both hemispheres and is well suited to visual learners.

A significant recent development in psychology is the concept E.Q. (Emotional Quotient) as opposed to I.Q. (Intelligence Quotient), where the realisation is that the former has not been given enough emphasis.

CHAPTER 8

Creative Study Methods

THIS chapter is a contribution from Mrs Lorraine Williams and re-flects some of her ideas relating to creative study methods.

It is a well known fact that children do not become more intelligent through reading and learning volumes of information. Rather, they become more educated through their 'connectedness' with knowledge. The important point is that the child has to own the information. It is this ownership of knowledge that changes the child's world-view and understanding of the objective world around him.

This ownership of knowledge allows the child to apply the knowledge intelligently and use it to his full advantage. The teacher needs to empower the child with this ability of being able to connect with this knowledge.

We will explore creative strategies that will help with the digestion of information and routines that will improve recall.

The key point is "GET CONNECTED" to the information.

SPIDERGRAMS

A **SPIDERGRAM** is a modern writing tool that enables one to take a quantum leap in creativity which in turn raises the standard of intellectual skills (ability to process information) by leaps and bounds.

The reason I recommend this format is because the spidergram is so visually attractive that the brain has an impulsive need to return to it. It activates the brain on different levels to become more agile and adept at learning and remembering. It is a creative method one can use to become connected to knowledge and at the same time experience some pleasure in processing the knowledge.

A **spidergram** is literally a web of information held together from a central point. It is a combination of words, codes, symbols and drawings held together in a pattern-web formation by the threads that radiate outwards from the central point.

The use of colour, images, codes and symbols help encode the information more strongly, making learning more effective and attaining goals that much less painful.

This format is completely opposite from that of linear notes whereby the eye has to process pages of sentences and paragraphs by following horizontal lines sequentially down the page.

However, when processing information in the spidergram format, the eye makes a completely different movement, it sweeps in a circular motion around the page, never losing sight of the whole concept. The more pleasurable the associations we have with learning, the easier it will be to process knowledge and the spidergram is by far more "learner friendly" than the linear mode.

APPLICATION
Summarising, note-making, description of spidergram

❏ MAIN HEADING in the centre of the page.

❏ SUB-HEADINGS branch off from the main headings. Each sub-heading has keywords chunked under it which are written on and below connecting lines and printed boldly and numbered in sequence.

❏ KEYWORDS are used instead of phrases/sentences written on and below connecting lines. Lines should be equal to the length of the word, instead of one long line.

❏ CODES-SYMBOLS-ILLUSTRATIONS along with words make it easier to process.

❏ COLOUR each chunk of information has its own colour which makes it orderly and not chaotic to process.

❏ CATEGORIES this orders information and reduces confusion.

❏ LAYOUT should be neatly presented.

❏ STYLE develop one's own.

ESSAYS

The brainstorming process is a highly creative and effective method of pulling random ideas together and then working them into some sequence.

Brainstorming in the spidergram mode helps us to move away from "starting at the beginning" and working sequentially through to the conclusion. We need to get away from sequential logic and reasoning, it doesn't allow for spontaneous exploration or expansion of ideas.

Step 1

Title in the centre of the page. Brainstorm ideas using one keyword at a time. Don't extend ideas into sentences at this point. Use the 5????? (five questions) where applicable, what, where, when, why and how.

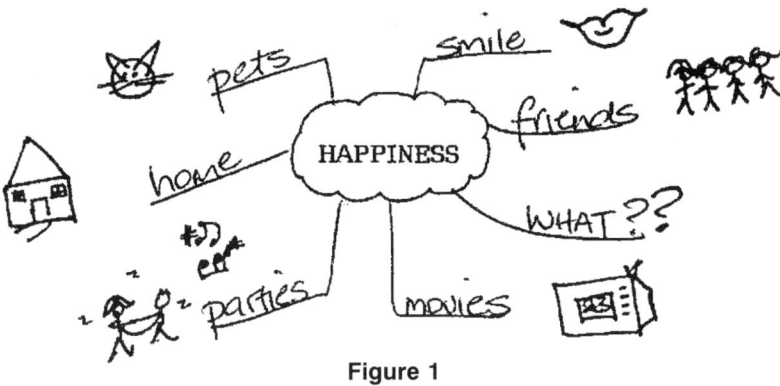

Figure 1

Step 2

Extend each idea and see if you can make a sentence. If there are any ideas that you can't use then don't add to them (e.g. Pets).

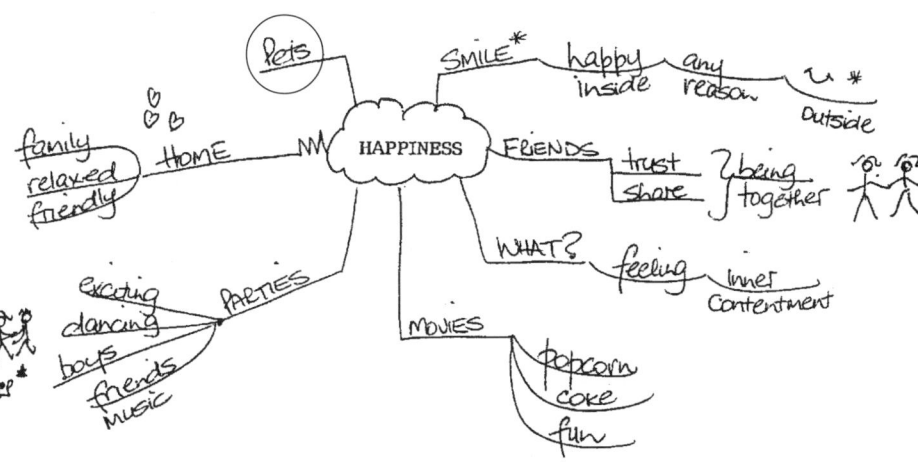

Figure 2

Step 3

Select/reject ideas and **number** them in sequence.

Step 4

Write the introduction and conclusion.

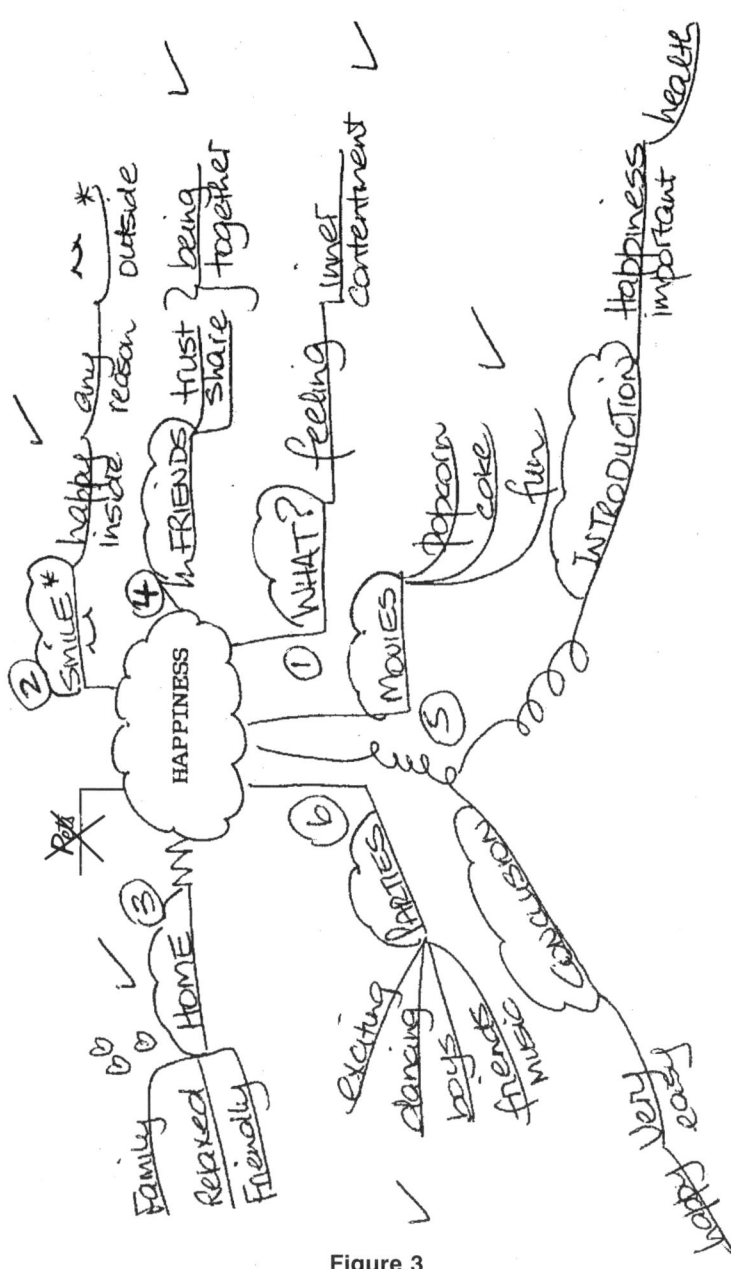

Figure 3

Step 5

Draft ideas neatly if brainstorming has become "messy". The sequence of ideas can still be changed at this stage.

CONCLUSION
Step 6

Write essay in linear form from the spidergram.

REVISION

Revision is one of the most important habits to develop. All information has to be revised to register in long term and short term memory.

We will never get away from rehearsal of information. If this pattern can be established in the classroom it will become a natural process.

We have to **SEE** it again, **HEAR** it again, **SAY** it again and **WRITE** it again.

PROJECTS

To include spidergrams as part of a project improves the presentation. Projects are expected to be creative and a combination of linear notes, graphs, illustrations, pictures and colour make the project not only aesthetically pleasing but greatly enhances impact.

BOOK REVIEWS

1. Title of book in the centre of the page.
2. Author
3. Introduction
4. Characters, part they play.
5. WHAT? story condensed & sequence of events
6. WHERE and WHEN it happened.
7. WHY and HOW it happened.
8. Vocabulary, pace, mood etc.
9. Conclusion (Comments such as, enjoyable, sad, moral, what did you feel)
10. Write in linear.

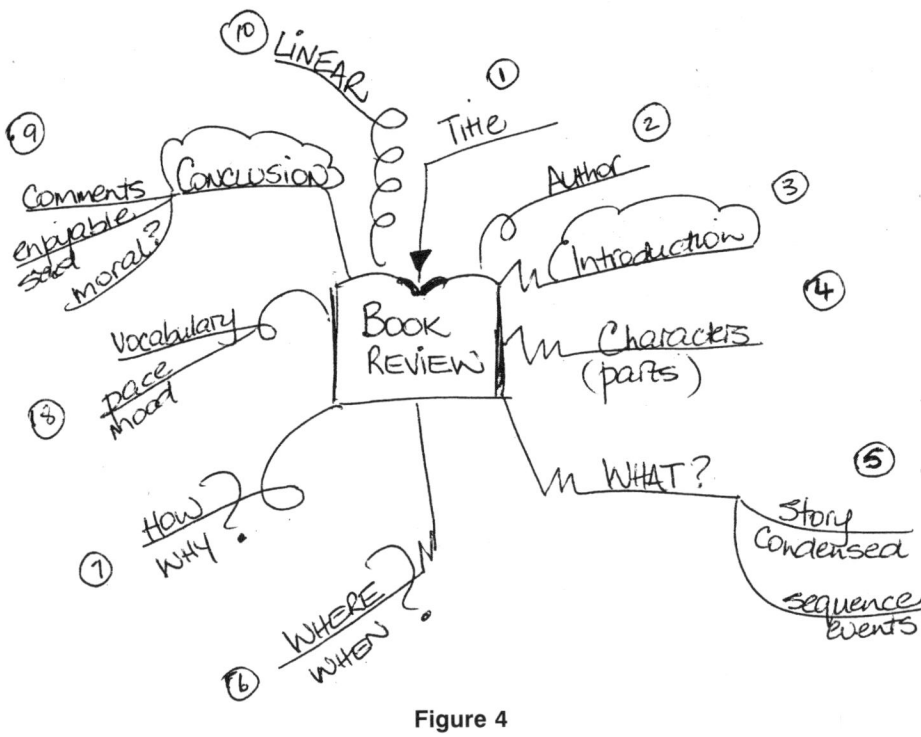

Figure 4

KEYWORDING

This is really one of the most important aspects of reading and looking for main keywords as it is a very active process.

The child has to be motivated, involved and interact with the information, otherwise it is just a passive exercise of looking at the words and glossing over the text. There are a few points we shall look at with regard to keywording to make it easier for the child.

IT IS NOT EASY TO LEARN/REMEMBER
FROM A CLEAN PAGE OF NOTES

There are a few easy creative steps to follow and once practiced a few times, makes keywording enjoyable.

A combination of techniques is recommended, such as hi-lighting a few of the main words with a koki pen and circling/squaring/coding words with a ball point pen.

Main points should be **numbered** and **listed** in the margin.

KEYWORDING

Spiders

Like scorpions and mites, spiders are **arachnids**.

They have two **2 parts** to their bodies, thorax and abdomen.

They have **8 legs** and if one breaks a new one grows during moulting.

They also have **8 eyes** and most spiders that spin webs don't see very well.

Underneath their abdomen they have organs which make silk called **spinnerets**.

The liquid (silk) is forced through tiny holes and becomes sticky as it reaches the air.

The spider spins it's **web** with this silk. This is home.

The silk is used to make diving bells, cocoons, traps and lifelines to save themselves.

They **live** in all manner of places indoors and outdoors, deserts, swamps, underwater and underground.

They may be all kinds of **colours**, brilliant red, yellow, green, grey, black or brown and can have striking patterns on their bodies.

S P I D E R S:

(1) Arachnids — Like scorpions and mites, spiders are (arachnids.) SMS   A

(2) — They have (2) parts to their bodies – (thorax & (abdomen. ta   2

(3) legs — They have (8) legs and if one breaks a new one is grown during moulting.   8

eyes — They also have (8) eyes and most spiders who spin webs don't see very well.

— Underneath their abdomen they have organs which make silk   S

(4) Spinnerets — called (spinnerets.)

— The liquid (silk) is forced through (tiny holes) and becomes sticky as soon as it reaches the (air.)   W

(5) WEB — The spider spins her (web) with this silk. This is home and the silk is also used to make (diving bells) cocoons, traps and lifelines to save themselves.

(6) LIVE — They (live) in all manner of places indoors and outdoors, (deserts, (swamps, (underwater & (underground. dusu   L

— They may be all kinds of (colours) – brilliant (red, yellow, green, grey black brown and can have striking (patterns) on their bodies.   C

(7) colours.

Figure 5

ELEMENTS OF LEARNING

Outline

Read

Say

Write

Revise

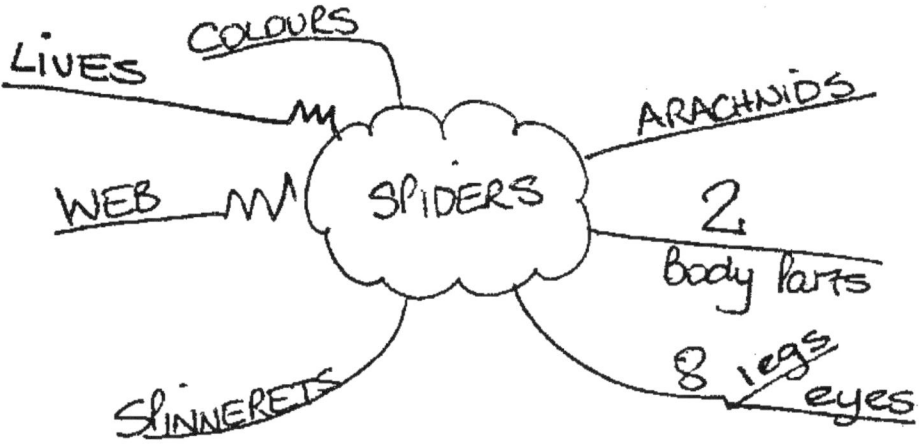

Figure 6: *Outline of headings*

1. The first step in learning is to hi-lite headings.

2. The second step is to write these down in a spidergram and learn them.

3. The third step is to draw the **spidergram** and learn the text. Incorporate **Read/Say/Write** while learning the text. Use visualisation.

The fourth step, once you feel you know the information, take a blank sheet of paper and try to reproduce the **spidergram**.

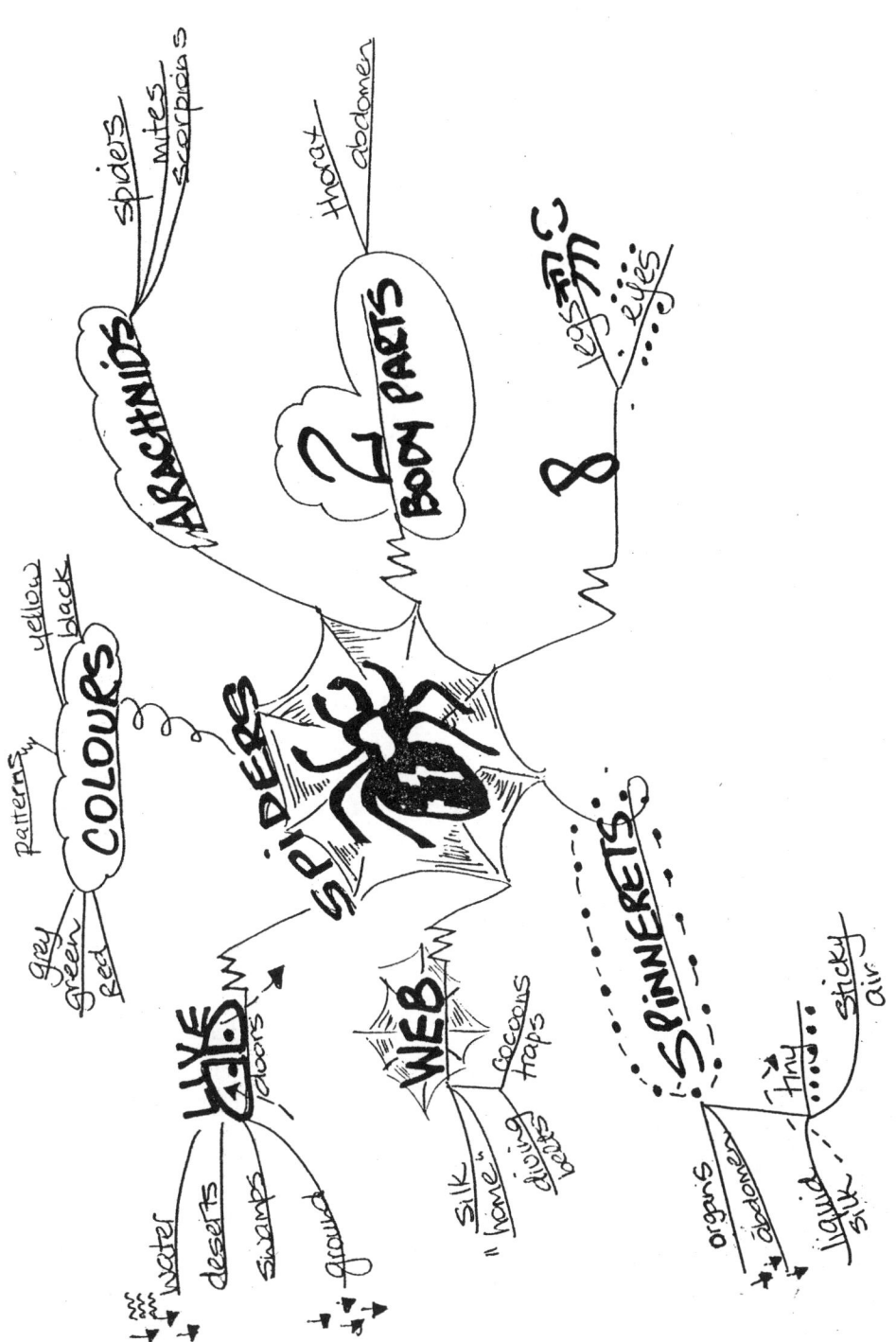

Figure 7: *Spidergram*

A revision is fast, messy, one colour and written in codes, symbols and initials, and less words. Start with the OUTLINE.

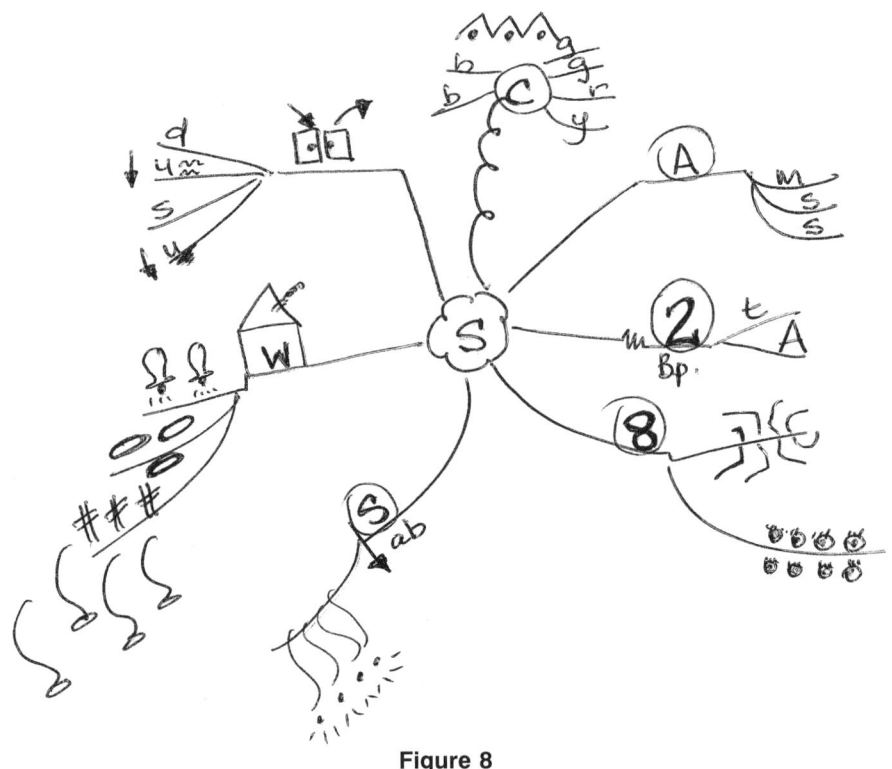

Figure 8

LEARNING STRATEGIES

	Options:	Spidergrams
		Linear notes
		Mnemonics

Spidergrams – First preference

After having drawn the spidergram –

Just **LOOK** at it.

Look at the images, codes, symbols, colours etc. a few times.

Now **LOOK** and **READ** together (LOOK to SEE, SAY to HEAR). Read it with meaning and **VISUALISE** the information as you SAY it.

When you think you know the information, take a blank piece of paper and write down the initials of the main points. Then go back to each initial (heading) and fill in the information, codes, symbols etc. In fact, it is sometimes easier to draw your images first and then fill in the words.

Linear Mode – second preference

Once the keywords have been found (marked, coded, squared, or circled) proceed as instructed for keywording.

The first step would be to make an outline (initials of headings) on blank paper and learn it.

The second step would be to learn the information from the linear text, ie, look and say the information to yourself, visualising it as you say it to make it meaningful.

Take a blank piece of paper and as quickly as possible try and reproduce the information in a **spidergram**, starting with the initials of headings first and then fill in the information.

If you have learned in linear mode then always revise the information back in a spidergram as fast as possible Outline first and detail second.

MNEMONICS

This is the art of improving memory. There are many systems designed to aid the memory. There are two things that have to happen when you learn information.

❏ You have to understand it.

❏ You have to remember it.

These are two different processes. Mnemonics improve the memory – quickly and easily.

If we use the text on **SPIDERS** for our exercise on memory we could use a couple of systems to recall that information. We could take the first initial of each heading and make a sentence, i.e. "A 28 yr. spider wears lavendar corduroys" – or we could simply make an acronym with the initials–

A 2 8 S W L C = 28 claws (mnemonic)

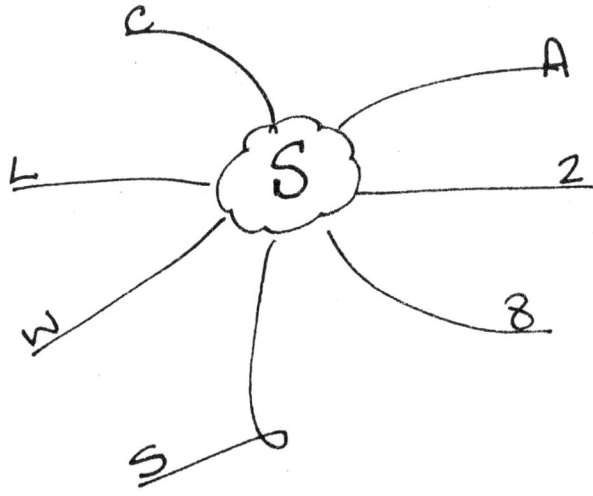

Figure 9

In remembering the mnemonic "A 28 yr spider wears lavendar corduroys" we visualise the picture and NOT the words. The picture needs to be recalled/revised regularly. Once we can remember the sentence easily then we decode its meaning

Memory training borders on the ridiculous, it is all pure imagination and fun. It does not aid the memory to use ordinary, or boring pictures. Images have to be ridiculous, stupid, crazy, bizarre, shocking, etc, then the pictures make a stronger impact. Memory training is to do with making an impact and the easiest way to do it is with imagery. Image memory is extremely powerful and frees one from the rigid rote learning mode.

NUMBER/RHYME SYSTEM

Each of the pegs/objects on the page 117 should be pictured vividly. The bun should be a specific kind of bun – Chelsea bun, cream doughnut, sesame bun, currant bun, etc. The shoe could be a pink ballet pump, a Doc Martin, a Caterpillar, a rugby boot. The tree could be a palm tree, fruit tree, a Christmas tree all dressed up. The door could be your front door, church door, temple door. The hive could be a glass box hive or a wild hive hanging off the side of the roof. Sticks could be a pile of brightly coloured large match sticks. Heaven could be an angel sitting swinging on the pearly gates, bait could be slimy, smelly squid. Wine could be red or white and hen could be this enormous speckled hen wearing sunglasses.

NUMBER/RHYME

1 BUN	
2 SHOE	
3 TREE	
4 DOOR	
5 HIVE	
6 STICKS	
7 HEAVEN	
8 BAIT	
9 WINE	
10 HEN	

Figure 10

Once we own this list we can use it again and again. We could use this list to remember our 7 headings belonging to SPIDERS. Don't forget we need to employ elements of humour to make strong impressions and that way we will remember the information more easily and for longer periods. So the elements we employ are – make the picture ridiculous, crazy, bizarre, shocking, etc. So here is the list – see what ridiculous, crazy pictures you can make:

Pegs   *Heading*
1. Bun – Arachnids (spider eating huge cream doughnut)
2. Shoe – 2 Body parts
3. Tree – 8 Legs/eyes
4. Door – Spinnerets
5. Hive – Web
6. Sticks – Live
7. Heaven – Colours

117

The list has to be revised regularly to hold it in long term memory. To recall the items in order recall the peg first and retrieve the heading associated with it (visualise the spider eating a huge cream doughnut). Second peg and 2nd heading used to make the picture, i.e.

recall bun   retrieve Arachnids

recall shoe   retrieve 2 etc.

REVISION ROUTINES

These are the learning habits that need to become regular routines.

1. Everything that is learned must have an **OUTLINE**.

2. Read, Say, Write, Revise

3. If learning from linear text, then **always revise information back into a spidergram**.

4. **REVISIONS** should be quick/messy/one colour Do as many as possible. Children with short term memories (they can't hold information for long) will need to do more revisions than children who can hold onto information for longer periods.

   If the short term memory learner does not do these revisions he will become extremely anxious because he cannot remember much and will also confuse information by putting it into wrong categories.

Revisions

1st   Ten minutes after new information is learned

2nd   At the end of the day

3rd   Next morning

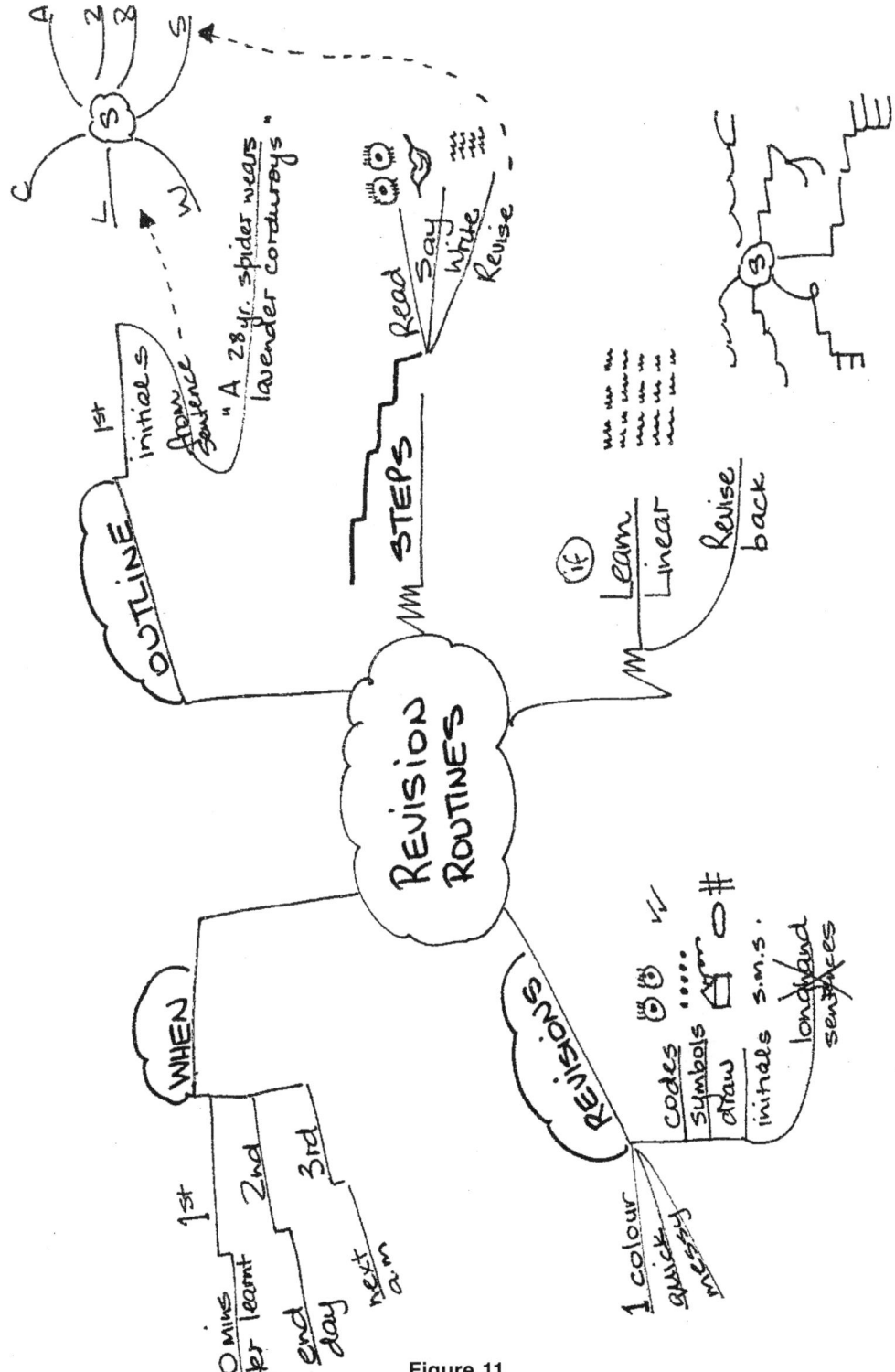

Figure 11

119

STUDY TIPS

1. It is easier to study in daylight hours. The light is natural and easier on the 'eye.

2. It is harder to learn late at night. The light is artificial and harder on the eye. Concentration diminishes as the evening wears on and energy levels become lower.

3. It is better to go to bed early and get up early, rather than going to bed late and getting up late. eg, in bed by 10 pm and up at 4 am, rather than bed by 12 pm and up at 6 am. The quality of sleep is deeper and more nourishing the earlier one goes to bed.

4 Check how music affects study. If the mind flicks from the work to the music, then attention will be split, in other words the music will be more charming than the work. Some children find Baroque music to be more restful.

5. Too much TV scrambles the brain! It is detrimental because it weakens all the good intentions and one ends up as a couch potato.

6. Learning breaks are essential. No one should be studying for hours on end without regular breaks. Most senior primary scholars can sit for about 30 minutes, high school pupils for 30 to 40 minutes and a seasoned honours student could sit for possibly 50 minutes at peak concentration plus being able to maintain motivation. As soon as the mind wanders, take a break. Learn for 30 minutes then break for 5 minutes. Do not study for 30 minutes and break for 30, this does not help concentration. Break for meals as well.

7. Try and reduce excessive caffeine intake at this time, (coffee/chocolate/coca-cola, etc.) it disturbs the balance of the nervous system. When learning, the most efficient/effective mode is when the mind is alert and the body is rested. Then the mind can absorb the information more efficiently and the body can digest it successfully.

TEACHING TIPS

Classroom Routine

❑ Start each lesson with a two minute revision of the previous day's module.

❑ Introduce the lesson.

❑ Outline the main points Spidergram.

☐ Teach the lesson: Discuss/Examples/Questions Spidergrams for each part on the board relate this part to the whole.

☐ Make mnemonic list.

☐ End with main points again (outline).

☐ Conclude with a quick two minute revision (class recall in spidergram format)

Weekly mnemonic lists could be constructed by the class.

Random Recall Excercises should be done on a regular basis.

Spidergrams or mnemonic lists.

Children should be given visual patterns to colour in, especially during double lessons to act as a buffer to left brain logic/reasoning.

It would also be good for the children to be engaged in random games of pictionary and other creative exercises.

Master Spidergrams should be constructed for all subjects. These could be done by the teachers or the pupils. If given to the pupils to construct it could be a group project.

All groups would have their tasks and targets and each child would have his own task to perform for the group. This becomes an excellent teamwork exercise.

Other motivating projects could be study groups that are formed. Tasks are given to the groups where they would have sections to prepare (spidergrams)/learn/teach to the group. Excellent exercise in expression/confidence/teamwork/time management.

BENEFITS OF SPIDERGRAMS IN THE CLASSROOM

1. They are visual and therefore elicit far more interest from the pupils.

2. They stimulate more group participation.

3. Lessons become more enjoyable and creative.

4. Far more creativity and spontaneity is generated by the teacher, allowing the pupils to become more involved.

5. The teacher's notes can become more flexible and adaptable over the years. The teacher is able to alter and add to teaching notes quickly and easily. This makes for very effective teaching.

6. The teacher is able to produce highly visual charts which can be laminated and used on an ongoing basis.

7. Spidergrams are very beneficial for class revision. A spidergram at the beginning and end of every lesson increases the child's ability to absorb/process/recall information more easily.

8. They improve the child's memory, both short term and long term.

9 The volume of information can be condensed into easily digestible portions.

10. Spidergrams are particularly useful for the child with learning diffi- culties. It frees the child from the "unreasonableness" of forever disecting/analysing and trying to find meaning and understanding in the linear mode, this often accounting for 90 % of the difficulty.

The spidergram allows the child a far more natural, spontaneous and creative expression of knowledge.

CHAPTER 9

The Left Hander

A S THE majority of left handers are right brain dominant, they are also visual learners and consequently the need to include this chapter in this guide is self evident. For centuries there have been many superstitions surrounding the left hander. It is common knowledge that there are many left handers who are talented, with special attributes, excelling in art and music and with some of the best known mathematicians, architects and sporting greats also being left handed. Working with many left handed children over a period of years, it has become apparent to the authors that there are still situations where they are permitted to use their left hand but are not always taught the left handed principles or afforded the same opportunities as their right handed peers.

Figure 1: *Remember they have a right to be left*

GUIDELINES FOR PARENTS AND TEACHERS

There are many parents and teachers who are eager to help and admit that the left hander should be afforded the same opportunity as the right hander but they themselves often lack the knowledge and skills needed to give them the right kind of instruction, guidance and support that they

123

need. Most educators recognise that children do not 'catch good hand writing' but have to be taught specifically to write. It is important to take into account that left handers are not only entitled to, but also have the right to be taught, as opposed to merely being permitted to use their left hand.

In her book, "Neuro-psychology of Left Handers", Jeannine Herron says, "Although left handers have often met with resistance, had their hands smacked, or even tied behind their backs, they did not just wither away and die. They survived. Why? because they do not choose their preference; they follow a neurological imperative".

There is a difference in teaching left handers and right handers and it should be taken into account that discrimination is not permissable on the grounds that left handers are the minority group. Parents and teachers will find it useful to familiarise themselves with a few facts about the left hander and the characteristics of left handedness.

❏ The difference that exists in the degree of hand usage in the general population is vast. Most research and literature seems to suggest that there are marked variations in the consistent preference for one hand and that the greatest consistent preference for using one hand only, is with learned skills and practiced tasks. The general tendency still is to judge a person's dominance on the basis of which hand is used for writing. In truth, some inherent "genetic left handers", who have for whatever reason, chosen to write with the right hand, may be ambidextrous because they have adjusted to living in a world designed for the right hander.

❏ The rights for lefts became a reality in the United States many years ago when ex-President Ford, who was himself a left-hander, started the "Bill of Lefts" where it is declared "That there will be no discrimination against left-handers in any field of endeavour or employment and that the welfare and dignity of the left-hander should be upheld at all times" (quoted from a Natal Mercury article written by the late Clarice Tucker), who was well known throughout South Africa for furthering the rights of South African left-handers. She was urging all right-handers to develop a better understanding of the problems that left-handers face. She also asked people to diarise and remember that August 13 of each year is International Lefty Day.

❏ Those whose names appear on the lefty list date back to Michael Angelo and Leonardo da Vinci. Other famous names include Ben Franklin, Charlie Chaplin, Ringo Starr, Paul McCartney, Marilyn

Monroe, Cary Grant, Judy Garland and Lewis Carroll. Great sportsmen include Ben Hogan, Mark Spitz, Martina Navratilova and Superbrat John Mc Enroe. Heading the South African list is Deputy President F W de Klerk. Others on the list are Carol Charlewood, Anton Nel, Barbara Anne Hawkes, and so the list continues.

THE DEVELOPMENT OF LATERALITY

The development of hand dominance does not appear to follow a definite or specific time schedule. It has generally been observed that babies from about four months onwards, when the two hands make contact, show a tendency to use both hands interchangeably and appear to be ambi-dextrous. From about three years onwards the tendency is to alternate dominance from one hand to the other until they are about six years old, during which a gradual shift to the preferred side is developed. Between the ages of six and nine years dominance should become strongly established. It is essential that a child should at least have established a preference for using one hand to write by the time he commences formal schooling. If doubt still exists regarding which hand is preferred for writing when formal schooling commences, it would be wise to seek professional advice from an occupational therapist.

GENETIC FACTORS IN LEFT HANDEDNESS

There are many genetic studies that have shown that the development of hand preference does have an hereditary basis. If the left-hander has no family history of left-handedness it is sometimes advisable to establish whether a physical disability or neurological deficit exists. However, there are certain environmental factors which do play a part in determining whether genetic left-handedness could perhaps be suppressed, as for example in certain cultures, where the development of left-handedness is not encouraged.

In their book, "The Left Handers World", by Dr Alvin Silverstein and Virginia B Silverstein, they said "There have been a number of studies that have indicated that left-handedness is hereditary. The results are, however, confusing because left-handedness does not follow the usual rules for the simple inheritance of traits". A team of Canadian researchers studied more than a thousand college students, some of whom were raised with their own parents and others with their step-parents. They found that right-handed parents were more likely to have right-handed children than left-handed parents but if the child was raised with the step-parents, the hand preference of the step-parents did not have any effect on the child's handedness. In other words, their handedness seemed to be determined by heredity rather than by learning.

Doctor Peter Behan, a neurologist at Glasgow University, said, "There is evidence that childhood learning disabilities, viz, dyslexia, autism, etc, occur predominantly in males and are increased among left-handers. It has also been established that dyslexia is at least fourteen times more common amongst left-handers than right-handers". Because of the enormous number of variables that exist, it is almost impossible to state with absolute certainty that the genetic factor is the only component in determining left-handedness.

THE INCIDENCE OF LEFT HANDEDNESS

There are no reliable statistics available of the incidence of left-handedness, the figure varying from 10 to 25 percent of the general population. For practical purposes it would be safe to say that in our schools we can expect to find that on average there will be three or four left-handers in every classroom. When the incidence is based on which hand is used for writing, most of the literature seems to show that there are twice as many left handed boys than girls. There does not seem to be a logical explanation for this occurrence but there seems to be a positive correlation between right brain dominance and left-handedness, with many boys showing right brain learning styles.

EYE AND HAND DOMINANCE

The significance and relevance of the relationship between eye and hand dominance has been discussed and researched, with the evidence again conflicting and outside the scope of this book. It has, however, been the practice to determine eye dominance in the left-hander in order to be able to advise the left-eye dominant left-hander to turn his paper more clockwise, to make it easier for him to see the work whilst writing.

To determine eye dominance, two checks are suggested:

Firstly, ask the child to point at an object approximately three metres away, then to close one eye to see if his open eye and finger line up. The left-hander is more likely to use his left finger to point and his left eye is more likely to line up. The child can also be asked to still focus on the object and close the other eye, when the object will no longer line up.

to perform the task. The usual response is for the left-hander to use his left hand and sight with his left eye.

GENERAL CHARACTISTICS OF THE LEFT HANDER

❑ He is known to make more left handed-free movements and gestures during conversation.

❑ There is a difference in limb size, with the left arm being longer and the left foot being larger.

❑ He usually has greater pain tolerance on the left side.

❑ His finger and palm prints are more symmetrical than those of the right-hander.

Some left-handers experience difficulty coping with conventions such as cutting with scissors and using rulers. In order to ensure that they learn to perform these types of activities with minimal stress, it is essential that careful individual instruction is given with the appropriate equipment, for example, a left-handed pair of scissors should be supplied. Be cautioned against purchasing the so-called 'ambi-dextrous scissors', as these are right-handed scissors which have more flexible blades but the blades are not reversed to ensure that the cutting line is exposed visually.

WRITING

The left-hander finds it more natural and comfortable to work from right to left and therefore shows a strong tendency to mirror write. The slope of the left-handers writing is not a natural forward slant and individual styles should be allowed to develop (as they will, if given time) an acceptable style of writing.

There are even some left-handers who prefer to angle their book to the right in order to achieve a natural forward slant, in the same way as the right hander.

Holding a pencil is often awkward for a left-hander, posture is poor and cramped arm positions are observed.

Left-handers are sometimes slow writers because they have an incorrect approach, resulting in a hooked hand position, with a tendency to press too hard, which leads to fatigue and contributes to slow writing.

The unconscious natural response for both left and right handers is always to move outwards from the body when writing, which happens to be the correct direction for the right-hander but not for the left-hander.

TEACHING LEFT-HANDERS

With individualised instruction, all left-handers should be able to achieve legibility and speed when writing. Applying the following suggestions will go a long way towards helping them achieve better results.

PAPER POSITION

At his first writing lesson he should be encouraged to sit to the right side of his desk, on the left side of the right-hander. His paper should be positioned on the left, with the right hand top corner nearer his body than the left, which allows free arm movement.

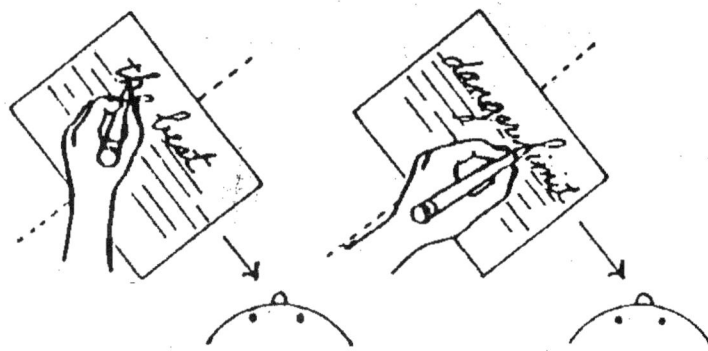

Figure 2: *Suggested hand position for the left-hander*

The degree of angle is an individual preference but it is essential to develop a comfortable angle to reduce the tendency to 'hook' and create the opportunity to introduce the slant into the writing with minimal effort.

This helpful quote is from Gardner's Manual of Instruction for the Left Hander, "Now study the position of your paper. At the left end of your first line of writing, your pencil will start far to the left. As you finish at the right edge of your paper, your pencil should still be slightly to the left of your mid-line".

If two children share a desk, ensure that the left-hander sits on the left side, with enough room to have his book to the left of the centre of his body. The right hand top corner of the page should line up with the centre line of the body.

PENCIL GRIP

In order to see what is being written, the pencil must be held at least three centimetres from the point, which is higher up the shaft than for the right-hander. A common failing with the left-hander is a tendency to grip the pencil very tightly which causes tension and fatigue. It could be helpful to wind a small rubber band around the pencil to stop the common tendency of letting the fingers slide down the shaft of the pencil. Where necessary, a pencil grip could be used to ensure that a mature tripod pencil grip is maintained.

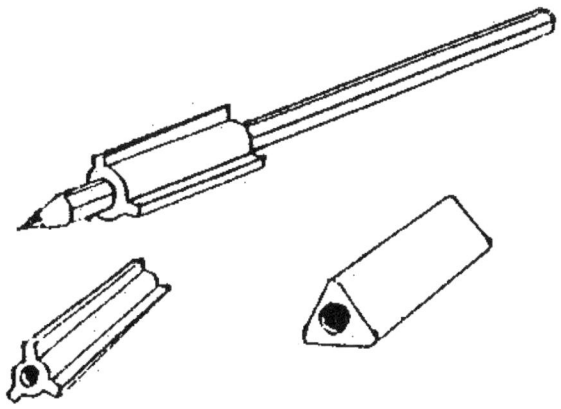

Figure 3: *Pencil grip*

TYPE OF PEN

Pens with broader, more flexible nibs should be used, an ideal pen is one with a bulbous end or a slightly turned up point. Special pens with reverse oblique points are commercially available and some ball point pens, for example, the roller ball type, are also suitable for left-handers.

LIGHT

Ensure that the light falls over his right shoulder to avoid shadows being cast onto his work.

ADDITIONAL CLASSROOM SUGGESTIONS

❏ The left-handers position in the classroom should be on the outside left to ensure that he does not constantly bump his right-handed partner.

129

❏ Because his book needs a greater angle and must be placed further from his body he may require more desk space than the right-hander.

❏ Ideally, initial writing practice should be on a blackboard as his hand will be below his writing and consequently he cannot 'hook'. He also has no restriction on his arm movements and has better control.

❏ Good results should be achieved if his teacher provides opportunity for practice of large writing on sheets of scrap paper.

❏ An important feature in teaching writing is to constantly emphasise correct starting points for letters and numbers.

❏ Constant reminders to keep his arm on, or to the left side of, the paper centre will ensure that his work is not covered and will help him achieve speed and fluency when writing.

❏ Teachers should be reminded that finger spacing is a concept which does not apply to left-handers and it is advisable to provide a small cardboard spacer for them.

❏ If the child reverts to the upright page position, try using Prestick to encourage him to work with his book at an angle. If there is resistance do not insist, but it is important to ensure that the book is well to the left of the mid-line of his body.

FACTS REGARDING THE HOOKED HAND POSITION

Inverted and non-inverted hand postures have been researched by Jerre Levy and Mary-Lou Reid, with details of their findings published in their book, "Left Brain, Right Brain", page 115 to 118, (see bibliography). In summary, they suggest that the inverted hand position (hooked posture), indicates that the language centre and preferred hand are controlled by the same side of the brain and consequently the hooked hand position reflects brain organisation, rather than being due to poor teaching techniques and incorrect angling of the book. The implication could be that the hooked pattern of writing in the left-hander may reflect left brain dominance. By the same token the hooked pattern observed in right-handers may reflect right brain dominance.

Although the original rigid belief that the left side of the brain controls the right side of the body and the right side of the brain the left side of the body, is a theory that still holds with many people, it is now known that there is a percentage of people who have other patterns of brain organisation, such as left-handers, who have left brain dominance and right-handers who show right brain dominance.

CAUTION

There is no doubt that more research is needed to substantiate findings such as those described above. The author has included this topic to stimulate an awareness amongst workers in the field who should be encouraged to liase with researchers to work towards finding solutions to help the children who have been labelled as having difficulties, when the reality is that there is still a lack of knowledge and insufficient facilities available to assist these children.

CHAPTER 10

Attention Deficit Disorder

IN THIS chapter the causes and major characteristics of ADD (attention deficit disorder) are outlined, together with intervention to improve both behaviour and academic performance. This topic is relevant here because right brain dominant visual learners present at school with ADD characteristics, although their attentional deficit is selective for listening skills and not for visual attention.

Epileptic children, even with effective seizure control, may have subclinical absences, particularly under stress such as in exams, which also reduces listening ability. Dr Gordon Serfontein's use of the term "THE HIDDEN HANDICAP" aptly describes ADD and is used appropriately for the title of his book.

DESCRIPTION

ADD is not a single condition but a manifestation of a cluster of symptoms and characteristics which interfere with learning and also impact negatively on the child's social adjustment. There are two categories of ADD, those with over-activity and those without over-activity.

Figure 1: *ADD children often over-react to common household noises*

The former category comprises disruptive, impulsive, physically restless, talkative, hyperactive children, whilst the latter comprises dreamers, who are often overweight, lethargic, unresponsive and allergic children.

Because young children are in general active and boisterous, they may be incorrectly described as having ADD. The distinguishing feature which sets the ADD child apart is the greater degree and frequency of the ADD behaviour which he displays, usually before the age of seven years. Often, as babies they do not crawl and later, they run rather than walk.

There are many symptoms, with five of the most pertinent ones being described here.

❑ An inability to maintain a sustained effort when working, and a tendency to move from one unfinished task to the next.

❑ Impulsivity, with an inability to stop and think before acting. Concepts that he should learn and apply are: "Look before you leap" and "Think before you ink".

❑ Physical restlessness, with an inability to sit still even when requested to do so. Non-stop chattering, which has no relevance to the task at hand, is also a feature of the syndrome.

❑ Listening skills are erratic with diminishing self-regulating behaviour. He has difficulty sticking to the rules.

❑ Inconsistency and variability in performance are greater than average. He has difficulty in achieving a balance between speed and accuracy when working, i.e. he is either too fast and makes a mess, or he is too slow and does not finish tasks in the alloted time.

BACKGROUND

ADD is not a new phenomenon. At the beginning of the present century it was thought to be a biological disorder. By 1990 it was considered hereditary and influenced by social circumstances.

It has had many labels, namely, Brain Damage Syndrome, Minimal Cerebral Dysfunction, Hyperkinetic Impulsive Disorder, Attentional Deficit Hyper-activity Disorder and Attentional Deficit Disorder.

It was first thought to be chronic and then that it would be outgrown by puberty. It is a developmentally disabling social conduct disorder with both biological and hereditary origins. Russell Barkley in his book, "Attention Deficit Hyperactivity Disorder", says, "Deficiencies arise early in childhood and are chronic in many cases; they are amplified by conditions of social disadvantage and predispose afflicted individuals to a high degree of social, educational and occupational under-achievement and to a lesser but still significant degree of anti-social conduct".

Barkley says that "the prevalence of the disorder is approximately 3 to 5 percent and occurs three times as often in boys as in girls, with the presenting symptoms being the same in both groups". The question is often posed, "Why more boys than girls?". Doctor Richard Haier, professor of paediatrics and neurology in Irvine, California, conducted research which supported the theory that the brain functions are different in men and women and that in women the corpus collosum is larger, enabling more efficient transmission between the left and right hemispheres and suggested that women are able to make more use of the language capacity of the right brain.

CAUSES

There is strong evidence for genetic factors, with brain injury accounting for a small number of cases. When it is genetic, the parents, because of their own similar problems, may find behavioural management difficult.

Hyper-activity occurs when the neurological system functions immaturely, often as a result of anoxia at birth (a lack of oxygen to the brain). It may also occur with neuro-chemical imbalance in the brain, or with thyroid abnormalities. The ascending reticular activating system (brain stem) may not inhibit incoming stimuli, auditory or visual, or outgoing motor movement and speech, which results in the child becoming distractible and restless.

CHARACTERISTICS

❑ The ADD child has difficulty controlling his own behaviour, following rules and anticipating consequences. Poor listening skills and a lack of comprehension in the classroom result in restlessness, frustration and poor motivation.

❑ His behaviour is often comparable to that of a younger child. He may be immature, aggressive and irritating and is therefore rejected by his peers.

❑ He is impulsive, defiant and disruptive, which results in under-achievement and antisocial behaviour.

❑ Low self-esteem leads to loneliness and even depression and maladjustment in later life. As an adult, his potential may not be fully realised in his career with a small but significant minority remaining anti-social. The majority, however, make a good adjustment, despite a history of scholastic underachievement.

Example:

Tom, who was not successful at school, is now a motivated person who has worked hard, using his right brain skills to become a successful training officer. His visual techniques enable his trainees, who are visual learners, to do well in their courses.

ASSESSMENT

Assessment measures must be selected to cover a variety of ages and ranges of behaviour. Several methods should be used including formal tests, questionnaires, interviews and observation.

Parents, teachers and the child should be interviewed. When rating scales are used it should be taken into account that they are subjective.

Appropriate intervention measures should be preceded by a full assessment to determine strengths and weaknesses, which should include measuring intellectual potential, determining levels of development of auditory, language and related skills, as well as levels of performance in visual perceptual and sensory motor areas.

INTERVENTION

Counselling, medication and diet are the three intervention measures to be described;

COUNSELLING

Barkley recommends family counselling to take the form of a parent training programme, with the objective being to teach the parents that ADD is partly an inborn biological condition, to which they must adjust, rather than to seek a permanent cure.

The way in which parents and families perceive themselves and the child can interfere with the implementation of a programme, and, in some instances, to their psychological adjustment to having an ADD child.

Co-operation with the teacher is essential and includes praising good behaviour and ignoring inappropriate behaviour. Incentives in the form of tangible tokens may be used, such as stars or rewards such as a smile, a hug, a positive comment.

Time Out (where the child is punished by being sent to a quiet spot on his own for a short period to cool off) is sometimes effective to reduce inappropriate and disruptive behaviour, both at school and at home.

School and home should co-operate, particularly to facilitate consistency, which is vital to acquire social skills.

Teachers should not punish the whole class when the child misbehaves, as this undermines him and reinforces his poor social adjustment with his peers.

The success of these procedures often depends on the teacher's ability to monitor the child's behaviour frequently and to provide immediate feed-back consistently, which is unfortunately difficult to achieve when the classes are large.

Maximum co-operation between the school, parents and the children is vital for these interventions to succeed.

MEDICATION

The stimulant Dexedrine (Amphetamine) was used until it was banned in South Africa, and Ritalin (Methylphenidate) has become the drug of choice. Although it is a stimulant for adults, it has the effect of sedating the child.

If the cause of ADD is organic or physiological, the medication is effective as it enables the reticular activating system to inhibit distracting incoming stimuli and restrict impulsive behaviour. However, there are side effects if taken over a long period, such as suppressing appetite and retarding growth but these are reversible when the medication is withdrawn. This is why it is sometimes given only on school days and not over weekends and holidays.

If side effects appear, the medication should be discontinued. As it takes effect within half an hour it is, in instances where the child leaves home very early, advisable for his teacher to administer the medication at school.

Ritalin is not usually prescribed for a child under the age of six years. As he matures neurologically his span of concentration lengthens and by adolescence his hyperactivity has usually been reduced to a level where medication is no longer needed. However, in some individuals the attentional deficit may remain.

It should not be used if tics are observed or if there is a family history of Tourette's Syndrome. It should not be used for children with epilepsy and it is advisable to have an EEG (Electroencephalograph) before the medication commences, as it may aggravate a pre-existing tendency to seizures.

Although research has not shown Ritalin to be addictive, using it over a long period of time could result in the child beginning to use it as a crutch, as he may feel that he cannot cope without it, in which case a placebo is suggested as a substitute.

Some children become emotional and tearful when the medication is initially taken and if these symptoms do not subside, the dosage should be discussed with the prescribing doctor.

Although there is a place for Ritalin for the child with learning disabilities, medication is not usually indicated for the visual learner, where a lack of concentration is a symptom and not the cause of the problem, the cause being poor listening skills, which will not be solved with medication.

A psychological assessment is advisable to identify whether the ADD symptoms have an emotional or psychological basis, in which case Ritalin will not be effective. Weekes and Collings, in a study of the management of Ritalin in the treatment of behaviour and learning disorders in children from junior primary to high school level, suggested that guidelines for the use of stimulant medication be followed, that it is used as a last rather than a first resort, and that facilities should be made available for evaluation, treatment and monitoring.

> When a child presents with ADD, which is a consequence of lack of discipline and structure, then teaching him self-regulating behaviour and introducing a routine at home would be more appropriate than prescribing medication.

Figure 2: *Discipline, not Ritalin*

137

Examples:

Ritalin was not effective for Conrad because an EEG revealed petit mal. When he was given anti-convulsant medication instead, his verbal score on the IQ test increased from below normal to average. He was then able to remain in the regular class, rather than being transferred to special education, which had been recommended.

A very positive response was that of Simon, whose ADD resulted in poor performance on the I.Q. assessment, excluding him from remedial school placement. Ritalin was prescribed and when he was reassessed his scores improved to the extent that he was accepted for admission to a remedial school.

A significant observation of these children was that their non-verbal IQ also improved, indicating that they were right-brain learners both with and without medication.

Some medical practioners prefer to prescribe Tofrinal, or other anti-depressants, to which children tend to develop a tolerance. Melleril, a tranquiliser, helps some children, especially those with aggression. Medication makes the child more manageable in the classroom and helps him to control his own behaviour. It is wise to ensure that the child knows why he is taking the medication.

DIET

Dietary management of ADD is a controversial subject and research has been inconclusive. Studies over the past decade have been based on small samples, over short periods of time, in laboratories rather than in normal situations and often on a single and possibly small amount of sugar or glucose.

Kruesi and Associates recommended reducing sugar intake because it replaces essential nutrients leading to under-nutrition. The United States Department of Agriculture outlined dietary guidelines in which it was recommended that sugar be used in moderation as an acceptable compromise.

Despite the lack of research evidence to substantiate the claim, there are many parents and teachers who report positive behavioural changes in hyperactive, ADD and allergic children whose diets have been adjusted. Many children have far more sugar than is necessary, in the place of more nutritious foods and would benefit from a more balanced diet.

Children may be lethargic or allergic but are more often hyperactive, thirsty, hungry and emotionally labile, resorting to tears and tantrums. When refined carbohydrates are reduced they seem to be less restless, irritable and aggressive, and more attentive.

Those children who have allergic rhinitis are perpetual sniffers. They tend to be slow, lethargic, unmotivated and concentration is poor. They are often the ones who have too much sugar in their diet. When their intake of refined carbohydrates is reduced they become brighter, more alert, motivated and the rhinitis clears up.

A medical doctor, who himself suffers with rhinitis claims that his rhinitis clears when he cuts down on his sugar consumption. He satisfies his sweet tooth with Canderel. In some instances dairy products are the culprit and not sugar. It is, however, clear that many children consume far too many refined carbohydrates and cutting down can only be beneficial.

Because sugar is a refined carbohydrate it is quickly absorbed, giving a burst of energy and then the blood-sugar level falls and hypoglycaemic symptoms may occur.

Figure 3: *Energy level rises . . .*

Figure 4: *then falls.*

A diabetic diet is suggested because, rather than being a weight control-ling diet, it is merely a healthy way of eating. A professsor of medicine once said that none of his family were diabetic but they were all athletic and followed a diabetic diet as a matter of choice because it is a way of eating that promotes good health (Appendix, page 149).

Figure 5: *The diabetic diet promotes good family relationships*

Tinned and other foods containing preservatives have as yet undeter-mined effects on health and behaviour; however, it is safe to say that as many unprocessed foods in the diet as possible is the way to go.

More research is required but avoiding junk food and refined carbohy-drates and developing better eating habits does seem to improve the be-haviour of some ADD children. It also brings more structure into the home, as the parents have to start taking control, particularly as the whole family is involved. The child should not be singled out and the dietary principles should apply to the family as a whole.

Example:

David, aged four, was described as having 'abominable' behaviour, but with a change in his diet, his behaviour improved dramatically. When he made the mistake of eating a slice of white bread and jam at school there was a sudden noticable deterioration in his behaviour. David has already learned to co-operate and eat more selectively because when he does so, he not only feels better but likes himself more.

CONCLUSION

Many children are described as having ADD, with the term being used loosely, in the same way that dyslexia is used to describe any learning problem, rather than a specific reading disability. The term ADD is often used to cover any problem in concentration, whether it be genetic or biological in origin, or as a result of a disorganised home environment, emotional problems or poor listening skills. A treatment method that suits one child may not be successful for another. It is therefore essential to begin with a full assessment to determine the best form of intervention for each individual child, which should include a rating scale (Appendix, page 154).

The opportunity to have a full assessment was not granted to Tom as a child. Now in adulthood he has been assessed and the findings have shown that he is right brain dominant with dyslexia. He is at present benefiting from the help he is having with a speech therapist. He explained the devastating effect of not having had that assessment in his own words as follows.

"Fifty three years of imprisonment, a self-made jail. The judges who confirmed my sentence that I was stupid, backward, were my school teachers, minister, friends, and the school psychologist recommended a school for the retarded.

"Dyslexia – it is not the spelling but the speller that has a problem; its not no brain but an unused brain.

"Now that I know why I can't read and write, the bars of my cell are not of steel, but only in the mind of an uninformed man.

"Thanks to my psychologist and my speech therapist my life is an open door to a new world to explore"

Tom has also written a poem which illustrates the desperation he felt at not knowing what was wrong with him –

"I know a man who had a song,
every time he sang, the words
came out wrong.

Every time he tried to repeat them,
the more it made him feel defeated,
he knew within that he was right
but did not know what was his plight.

How can he ask for loving care
if he did not know the problem was
there"

CHAPTER 11

Conclusion

THERE is a need to emphasise that with the enormous amount of research and literature available on right brain dominance, the concept that it is imperative for teachers and parents to know whether their children are right or left brain dominant, has become fashionable. However, it is vital to guard against the danger of losing sight of the real issue, namely,

LATERAL BRAIN INTEGRATION (using both hemispheres)

To function in an integrated state, the child needs bilateral integration, with access to both hemispheres at the same time, with both ears, both eyes and both sides of the body (switched on). A laterally integrated child is one who has learned to use two sides together as a whole system, the left and right brain working in an integrated fashion through the corpus callosum.

Homo-lateral functioning reduces the joy of movement. We reiterate that we cannot over-emphasise the importance of movement in learning, the laterally integrated child is one who is able to process information simultaneously with both hemispheres. He can move and think at the same time, read with the writer's hand and speak with the listener's ear. The integrated child thrives on the new, the spontaneous, the creative. Every task, complex or simple, becomes a joyful opportunity for full expression.

Many educators have stressed the need for integrating left hemisphere/ right hemisphere thinking in education. We endorse this concept in the hope that policy makers will make the much needed adjustments to the system.

From the authors:

Our aim has been to offer support to visual learners and their parents by suggesting methods and strategies to cater for a range of learning styles. By implementing these suggestions they should begin to achieve in their own way by building on those right hemisphere skills where they already have competence, and use them as an entry point into our left hemisphere dominated world. In our wonderful country with its diversity of cultures and many languages, there surely is no better way to go than,

THE RIGHT WAY

Appendix

ACCELERATE PRE-SCHOOL ENRICHMENT PROGRAMMES

These programmes have been written for parents to use with pre-schoolers in the home setting, using readily available items to develop basic skills for school readiness.

The programmes are also suitable for use with older children, who for one reason or another, have difficulties in learning and require stimulation in basic skills. They can be used as a valuable addition to a remedial programme by teachers and therapists as well.

Each programme consists of a basic checklist, with norms for age levels 3–6 years. The daily programme provides graded activities, with five activities per week for six weeks.

A "Comments and Discussion" note at the end of each day's activity gives the parent/teacher more in-depth information regarding the importance of the activity. It also provides guidelines to assess the child's functioning with that day's activity. A weekly checklist guides the user in how well the child is coping with the programme.

ACCELERATE Level One is suitable for use with children 3 years and older. It is recommended that all six programmes be used in the order that they are presented, i.e.

BOOK ONE: BODY IMAGE – Rita Edwards

Provides daily activities to develop knowledge of body parts and their functions, size and form of body, and spatial concepts of the body. It also provides a number of games and creative activities that can be used to develop an awareness of the body.

BOOK TWO: MOVEMENT SKILLS PROGRAMME – Rita Edwards

Movement is as fundamental a need for every child as eating and sleeping. This programme provides daily activities to develop balance and posture, gross and fine motor co-ordination and bilateral integration.

BOOK THREE: LANGUAGE PROGRAMME – Linda Cohen

Language is the basis of communication. This programme is designed to enhance the pre-school child's language skills in concept development, categorisation and receptive and expressive language.

BOOK FOUR: BODY-SPACE INTEGRATION – Rita Edwards

Once the child has a well-established concept of how his body looks (Book 1) and how he can use it (Book 2) the child is ready to learn how to use his body in his wlorld; i.e. body-space integration. In this programme, the child learns to relate body parts to each other and the space around him, as well as identifying sides of the body and on objects (left and right). This child also learns to identify directions of movement, an importnat basis prerequisite for learning to write and draw.

BOOK FIVE: VISUAL PERCEPTUAL PROCESSING PROGRAMME – Rita Edwards

These daily activities will enhance and enrich the child's perceptual processing skills, specifically in visual discrimination, perceptual constancy of form, size, colour and number, as well as part-whole perception.

BOOK SIX: AUDITORY PERCEPTUAL PROCESSING – Linda Cohen

These activities are designed to provide the child with daily exercises in listening skills for auditory discrimination, localisation of sounds, listening for meaning and identification of sound.

Mrs Rita Edwards
P.O. Box 26347
Hout Bay
7872
Tel (021) 7629138

AUDIO TAPES FOR LEARNING MATHEMATICAL TABLES

Pat Strachan, a remedial specialist, has devised a tape called Number Rap for learning tables. It is accompanied by a booklet which should be followed whilst listening to the tape. This method of using rhythm in rote memory is fun and particularly beneficial to right brain learners. The tape and booklet can be obtained from:

> Mrs Pat Strachan
> 259 Queen Elizabeth Avenue
> Manor Gardens, 4001
> Telephone (031) 811 825

CREATIVE STUDY METHODS

Creative study methods seminars enables pupils to use both sides of the brain, instead of only a small percentage, which learning generally directs to the left brain. The right brain responds to art, music and patterns, processing information more holistically and grasping the picture quickly, while the left brain tends to work on a step by step basis, responding to words and meaning.

Creative study methods utilise right brain skills and ensures the use of both hemispheres in an enjoyable manner which is beneficial at both school and tertiary levels.

For more information contact:

> Lorraine Williams
> P O Box 634
> 3640 Kloof
> Telephone/Fax (031) 764 3775

EDUCATION IN HUMAN VALUES

Moral and spiritual development are missing factors in the educational system. Education in Human Values fills this gap for children between the ages of six to fifteen years. Parents with teenagers have found it effective in overcoming problems experienced by their children. The techniques have been found to make a positive change emotionally in children who are not speaking, or have emotional problems and become demoralised and lacking in confidence. They instil a sense of well being and should have a healing effect on, for example, children of violence.

The five human values are Truthfulness, Righteousness, Love, Peace and Non-violence. They can be integrated into classroom subjects such as, language, maths, science and social studies and included in activities outside the classroom in games, sport, debate and drama.

The techniques, which use right brain skills are:

1. Silent sitting or tuning in, which enables the right brain to take over from the left and is useful before studying with visual learning methods. It takes only a few minutes and leads to better concentration, receptivity, grasping power and memory.
2. Prayer or quotations. Prayers are used in school assemblies and promote tolerance and respect for others. They use memory, melody and meaning.
3. Group singing. The children enjoy this and feel good. Memory improves and they feel a sense of peace, love and appreciation. Anything learned through song and music remains in the memory longer and is easy to recall.
4. Story telling. This is effective in driving home any message and bringing out parallel situations in life, suggesting solutions. It adds colour and variety to the school situation and has an impact on childrens' conduct. Pictures should also be used.
5. Group activities such as motivational games, drama and role playing. Children are dynamic by nature and teachers can streamline their energies, instilling a sense of discipline and feeling of co-operation.

Contact person:

Mrs J Singh

12 Fiddlewood Drive
4110 Isipingo Hills
Telephone: (031) 902 4562

FUNKEY CARDS

These are multi-sensory card games using auditory and visual perception, devised by a remedial teacher to teach phonics to children with reading problems and reluctant learners. They may be used by teachers, remedial teachers, therapists, parents and children and are played in the same way as conventional card games such as Happy Families, Old Maid, Snap and Rummy.

The cards are laminated with lively cartoon style drawings which appeal to children. They can be used to teach tricky two letter sound combinations such as; *oa ea ai au* and *ou,* as well as consonant blends such as: *fr br sl sm scr str,* and the final *e.*

They are available from some specialist book shops, educational shops or from Mrs Tricia O'Brien, who designed them. Her address is:

P O Box 379

Petervale, 2151

Telephone (011) 706 3396

JUMP SHEETS

In this fun way of teaching, using movement, designed by Dr Alexander Bannatyne, the teacher prepares jump sheets using pieces of plain white material (sheeting). She makes a nine block grid on the sheet, where each block is big enough to allow the child to jump comfortably onto the block with both feet.

The middle block is blank, or feet are drawn onto it representing the starting point. The surrounding blocks are prepared according to the lesson requirements as shown in the diagram below.

The example sheet is designed to teach the *ea* sound as in the following words: *read, each, beat, team, beach, meat, lead, bead, cheat*, etc.

It is not always necessary to number the blocks but it may help direct the younger child to the correct block when errors occur.

Procedure

The teacher, or mother, says the word which has all its letters printed onto the sheet. For example meat. The child stands on the middle block and jumps with both feet onto block 7 (m), saying the sound out aloud as he jumps onto the block. He then jumps to block 2 (ea), saying 'ee', then onto block 6, sounding out the 't'. Finally, he jumps back onto the middle block says the whole word, meat, as he lands.

Do not assume that he has recognised that the word has four letters but only three sounds. He must understand that that the *e* and *a* are said as one sound.

A group spelling game can be arranged with two teams where a member of the first team jumps from block to block to spell out a word, whilst the other teams members must recognise and call out the word. If the second team does not recognise the word, or says an incorrect word, they lose a turn.

These blocks can be drawn onto the floor with chalk but the advantage of the sheets is that they can be time savers, as they are pre-prepared and can also be cleaned and stored away easily. The innovative teacher will recognise the opportunity to prepare sheets to teach an almost unlimited variety of concepts and skills, which include shapes, numbers, listening, spelling, grammar, sentence construction, etc.

REDUCED CARBOHYDRATE DIET

This is not a weight reducing diet. It is intended for children who do not have balanced, nutritious meals and who consume an excessive amount of sugar. It has been vetted by a dietician and is based on a diabetic diet, which is a healthy way of eating and suitable for the whole family. It is not suitable for those who are allergic to dairy products, eggs or gluten, for whom modifications would be required.

A good breakfast is essential to keep up energy levels at school and it is important to have fibre. For a balanced diet items from the five categories should be included daily, viz, protein, fruit and vegetables, grains, starches, fats and oils.

Meals should be on time and the child should not go hungry or thirsty. He can snack on, for example, Provita biscuits, cheese, a stick of carrot, dry cereal (not sugar coated), plain popcorn, nuts or a wholewheat bread sandwich. Water is a good thirst quencher.

Suggested foods to avoid

Sugar (white, brown, castor, icing), honey, syrup, jam, marmalade, glucose. Caffeine, coffee. Sweets, chocolates, preserved fruit, dried fruit, raisins. White flour (in bread, cakes etc.). Tomato sauce, soya sauce, chutney. Tinned spaghetti in tomato sauce, baked beans in tomato sauce, fruit in syrup, sweetcorn. Cakes, biscuits, puddings, custards, condensed milk. Flavoured yoghurt (except with sugar). Ice cream and jelly (except diabetic jelly). Flavoured milk, fizzy drinks, sugar based squashes, diet cold drinks (except diabetic), soda fountain drinks. Grape juice, prune juice, blackcurrant extract, wine. Sugar coated cereals, honey crunch, honey wheat, cream cracker biscuits, water biscuits, matzos (except wholewheat).

In moderation

Tea, mayonnaise, salad dressing. Bananas, apples. Processed meats. Over-the-counter medication with caffeine, glucose, syrup base.

Suggested foods allowed

Slow release sugars, seminola based pasta, brown rice. Milk, plain yoghurt. Fresh fruit (except grapes, plums, prunes). Vegetables. Wholewheat breads and biscuits, rye bread. Oats, mealie meal, beef and vegetable extracts, fish paste, plain potato crisps, soda water, herbal tea, tinned fruit (without sugar), meat, poultry, fish, margarine, butter, oil, cheese, cottage cheese, nuts, popcorn. Artificial sweeteners so that he can still have the benefit of a sweet taste.

Once the child's craving for sugars has been lost he should be less hungry and thirsty and behaviour should improve. Concentration and allergic rhinitis also often improve.

A healthy diet, with everything in moderation, should be followed. Sweets are permissible on occasion, as treats, perhaps over week-ends. The child should feel better and he should not be allowed to over-indulge again.

SITTING POSTURE AND PENCIL GRIP
How to sit at your desk

Lean forward a little but do not lean on the desk.
Your head should not be too near your paper
or exercise book.
Your feet should be flat on the floor.
Sit right in front of your desk. Do not lean to
the side.
Your elbows must not rest on the desk.
The end of your pencil should point along
your arm.
Do not sit stiffly at your desk. Be comfortable
so that your hand and arm can move quickly
and easily.

WRONG POSITIONS

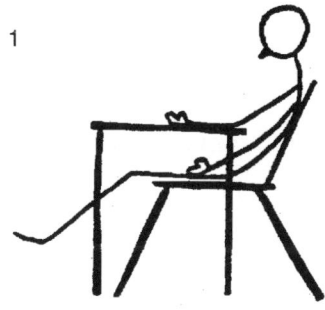

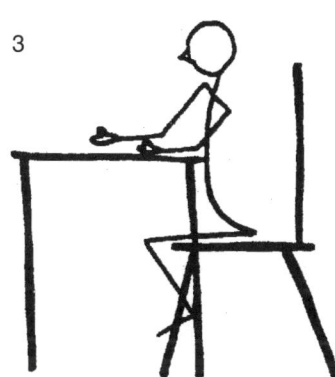

How to hold your pencil

Hold your pencil very lightly with your thumb and forefinger. Your middle finger should also rest very lightly on the pencil. Your other fingers and your hand can rest lightly on the desk.

Do *not* press heavily on the paper.

The pencil should point along your arm. It must not point up in the air or towards your body.

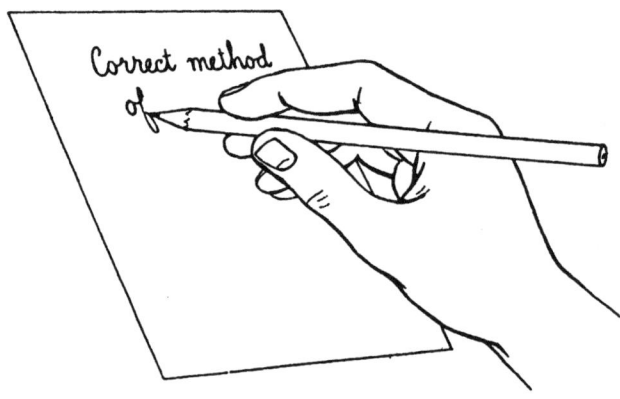

Comfortable pencil grip and paper position for the right hander

CHECKLIST FOR TIMED HAMMERING SAMPLE

Child's name .... Age .... Date of Birth ....

	Date test one..........		Date test two..........		Date test three..........	
	1st sample	2nd sample	1st sample	2nd sample	1st sample	2nd sample
Which hand was used? Indicate L or R						
Number of strikes						
Number of attempted transfers L to R						
Number of attempted transfers R to L						
Hand grip. (tick appropriate column) weak						
fair						
strong						
Arm and hand function (tick appropriate column)						
(a) wild, uncontrolled, poor visual attention						
(b) barely adequate, skidding, off target						
(c) well directed response in arm and hand						

Additional observations (comment below)

....

CHECKLIST FOR ATTENTION DEFICIT DISORDER

MODIFIED CONNOR'S ABBREVIATED TEACHER

Rated Symptom Qestionnaire
Name of child ....
Name of teacher ....
School ....
Date of observation ....

	Not at all 0	Just a little 1	Pretty much 2	Very much 3
1. Restless or overactive				
2. Excitable and impulsive				
3. Disturbs other children				
4. Constantly fidgets				
5. Untidy, handwriting poor, uneven				
6. Inattentive, easily distracted				
7. Demands must be met immediately– Easily frustrated				
8. Fails to finish things he started– Short attention span				
9. Daydreams, cannot get started on work by himself, needs constant supervision to finish				
10. Does not mix well – has few friends				
11. Cries easily and often				
12. Mood changes quickly and drastically				
13. Temper outbursts, explosive, unpredictable or aggressive				
14. Isolates himself from other children (Ritalin overdose effect)				
Total				

Dear Sir,

The parents of this child have been asked to approach you to obtain the information indicated on this form to act as a guide to diagnosis and management of this child's problems. This direct approach has the approval of the director of education.

Thanking you in anticipation.

Yours sincerely,

....

The class teacher

The words marked in yellow are applicable to this form.

Please complete form No. 1 on date indicated (please write in date of actual completion).

Keep other forms until you receive a further request from me indicating on what dates they are to be completed and returned.

This child is suspected of having a learning problem/a conduct disorder/hyperkinesis.

1. I have seen the child and obtained a history from the family, but to get a more complete history we would be obliged if you could complete the questionnaire on the date indicated.

2. The child is now on medication.

3. The does of medication has recently been changed.

Please do a repeat assessment to establish effect of medication.

Use this space for any other information or comment that you consider helpful and informative.

LETTER AND NUMBER FORMATION AS TAUGHT IN NATAL SCHOOLS

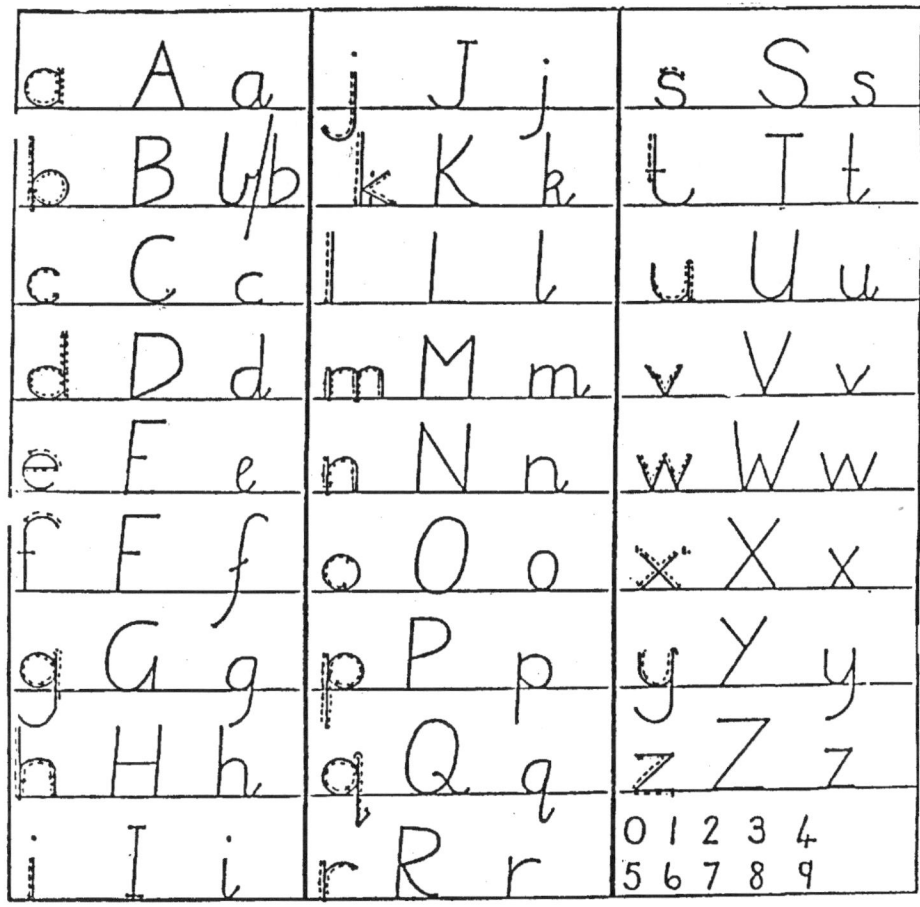

a	A	a	j	J	j	s	S	s
b	B	b	k	K	k	t	T	t
c	C	c	l	L	l	u	U	u
d	D	d	m	M	m	v	V	v
e	F	e	n	N	n	w	W	w
f	F	f	o	O	o	x	X	x
g	G	g	p	P	p	y	Y	y
h	H	h	q	Q	q	z	Z	z
i	I	i	r	R	r	0 1 2 3 4		
						5 6 7 8 9		

Bibliography

BANNATYNE, Alexander. Language, Reading and Learning Disabilities. Charles C Thomas. 1976.

BARKLEY, Russell A. Attention Deficit Hyperactivity Disorder. The Guildford Press. 1990.

BEGLEY, Sharon. Gray Matters. Newsweek CXXV(13). 27 March 1995. p 42-48

BENTON, David. Dietary Sugar, Hyperactivity & Cognitive Functioning: A Methodological Review. Journal of Applied Nutrition. 41 (1). 1989

Caroline, Sister Mary. Breaking the Sound Barrier (A phonics Handbook). The Macmillan Company. 1960

DONALDSON-SELBY, Claudia. Write Way Up. 2 Berkley Street, Oranjezicht, 8001

DENNISON, Paul. Switchin on. Thom C Hawley R.S.A. 1990.

EDWARDS, Betty. Drawing on the Right Side of the Brain. Souvenir Press. 1979

EDWARDS, Rita. Accelerate Pre-School Enrichment Programmes. Sigma Press. November 1990.

GARDINER. Left-handed Writing.

GESELL, Arnold. The Child from 5 Five to Ten.

GRAHAM, Philip. Hyperactivity & Diet. Nutrition & Food Science. March/April 1987.

HORNSBY, Beve. Overcoming Dyslexia. Juta & Co 1984.

ISRAEL, Lana. Brain Power for Kids. Hippo Communications 1991.

ISRAEL, Lana. Another Angle. Hippo Communications 1993.

KNICKERBOCKER, Barbara. A Holistic Approach to the Treatment of Learning Disorders. Charles B Slack 1980.

KRUESI, Markus & Others. Effects of Sugar and Aspartame on Aggression and Activity in Children. American Journal of Psychiatry. November 1987.

LIVING & LOVING. April 1994

LOWENBERG, Elaine L. An Investigation into Specific Learning Disabilities Possibly Associated with Dysfunctions of the Tempor-Parietal Lobes in the School-Going Child. Doctoral Dissertation. December 1976.

LOWENBERG, Elaine L. Specific Language Disability – A Medical or Educational Problem. South African Medical Journal. 26 November 1986.

LOWENBERG, Elaine L. Specific Language Disability – The Cinderella Remedial Problem. SAALED Congress Proceedings. 1984

LUCAS, Elsie M. Learning Difficulties in Learning Disabilities in your Child. Edge, Wallace & Loening. Juta & Co. 1976.

LUCAS, Elsie M. You Have a Right to be Left. T C Tuck 1990.

MACFARLANE-SMITH, I. Spatial Ability. University of London Press. 1964

MIMS DESK REFERENCE. 1994.

MULLER, Beverley & MTHETHWA, Bongani. Sanibona I. Noel Glass Press. 1982.

MURPHY, K.V.N. The Greatest Adventure. Sri Sathya Sai Publications.

OSTRANDER, Sheila & SCHROEDER, Lynn. Superlearning. Souvenir Press. 1979.

POPE, Jill. The Brain's Emergence Towards Human Values. Fall 1987.

ROSEN, Lee & Others. Effects of Sugar (Sucrose) on Children's Behaviour. Journal of Consulting & Counselling Psychology. 56(4)1988.

ROSNER. Jerome. Overcoming Learning Difficulties. Walker & Co. 1985.

SERFONTEIN, Gordon. The Hidden Handicap. Simon & Schuster. 1991.

SPRINGER, Sally & DEUTSCH, Georg. Left Brain, Right Brain. W.H. Freeman & Co. 1981.

SWERDLOW, Joel I. National Geographic. 187 (6) June 1995. p 2-41.

TURNBULL, D. K. A student's Introduction to Visual Science & Optometry. University of Durban-Westville 1993.

VITALE, Barbara Meister. Unicorns Are Real. Jaimar Press 1982.

WEEKES, D.S. & COLLINGS, S.J. The Use of Methylphenidate in the Treatment of Childhood Behavioural and Learning Disorders. A Replication & Extension. South African Journal of Education 14(1) 1994.

WITELSON, Barbara. Dyslexia: A Hemispheric Explanation. Science News, Vol 111. 1977.

WOLRAICH, Mark & Others. Effects of Diets High in Sucrose or Aspartame on the Behaviour & Cognitive Performance of Children. New England Journal of Medicine. February 3, 1994.

WOO, Elaine. Teaching That Goes Beyond IQ. Los Angeles Times. May 1995.

ZAIDEL, Eran. Language in the Right Hemisphere. The Dual Brain. Guildford Press 1985.

Index